A complete

Physical Education

Program

for the entire family without competition

Alexander D. Marini

Noble Publishing Associates

P.O. Box 2250

Gresham, Oregon 97030

(503) 667-3942

Noble Publishing Associates, the publishing arm of **Christian Life Workshops,** is an association of Christian authors dedicated to serving God and assisting one another in the production, promotion and distribution of audio, video and print publications. Write or call us for instructions on how you may participate in our association, or for information about our complete line of materials.

© 1994 by

Alexander D. Marini

ISBN 1-56857-017-1

9 781568 570174

Printed in the United States of America

ABOUT THE AUTHOR

Alexander D. Marini has been involved in physical fitness and athletics since his boyhood. He received a Bachelor of Science in Physical Education from Springfield College, Massachusetts, in 1978. Alex currently holds state teacher certification in the field of Health and Physical Education in both Massachusetts and Pennsylvania, as well as YMCA certification as a Physical Fitness Specialist and Youth Sports Director. He has worked as a teacher and coach in public and private schools, and YMCAs; and he home schools his own children. Alex presently resides in New Holland, Pennsylvania, with his wife, Susan, and five children, Dena, Joanna, Anthony, Paul and Emily. He and his family are active members of Charity Christian Fellowship, Leola, PA.

To the Parents

In my years of teaching physical education in schools, YMCAs and at home, I have always felt privileged to be the gym teacher, as it gave me the opportunity to develop a unique relationship with my students. I saw them (and they saw me) from a different perspective than all their other teachers, since I made it my practice to participate with my students whenever possible.

When you decided to home school, you chose to go all the way with parenting, taking on the full God-given responsibility for the training of your children. I want to commend you for making that choice, and I want to encourage you to include Physical Education in that choice: exercise with your children, practice with them, work and play with them. After all, you need exercise too, and probably more than your children. But beyond that, don't miss out on the opportunity to develop this unique aspect of your relationship with your children, and to be a good example to them in working, succeeding, failing, persevering and maintaining God's temple. God's blessings to you.

Alexander D. Marini

Table Of Contents

Preface vii

Acknowledgements viii

How To Use This Manual ix

PART 1: PHILOSOPHY

Chapter 1. A Biblical Basis 3
Chapter 2. Goals. 7
Chapter 3. Philosophy of Games 9

PART 2: PREPARATION

Chapter 4. Planning Your Program 17
Chapter 5. Equipment 31

PART 3: PHYSICAL FITNESS

Chapter 6. General Fitness Principles 35
Chapter 7. Aerobic Exercise 37
Chapter 8. Strength Exercise 43
Chapter 9. Flexibility Exercise 57

PART 4: ACTIVITIES

Chapter 10. Skill Development 63
Chapter 11. Work Activities 65
Chapter 12. Activity Units 67
Chapter 13. Game Organization 69
Chapter 14. Badminton Unit 71

Chapter 15. Baseball Unit 73

Chapter 16. Basic Ball Skills Unit 77

Chapter 17. Basketball Unit 85

Chapter 18. Chase Games Unit 89

Chapter 19. Field/Gym Day 93

Chapter 20. Football Unit 95

Chapter 21. Frisbee Unit 101

Chapter 22. Gymnastics Unit 105

Chapter 23. Hand/Eye Coordination Unit 119

Chapter 24. Handball Unit 121

Chapter 25. Locomotor Skills Unit 123

Chapter 26. Obstacle Course Unit 127

Chapter 27. Paddleball/Racquetball Unit 129

Chapter 28. Pillow Polo Unit. 131

Chapter 29. Ping Pong Unit 133

Chapter 30. Relay Races Unit 135

Chapter 31. Soccer Unit 139

Chapter 32. Swimming Unit 143

Chapter 33. Tennis Unit 157

Chapter 34. Tetherball Unit 159

Chapter 35. Track and Field Unit 161

Chapter 36. Volleyball Unit 165

In Closing 169

Bibliography 171

PREFACE

Physical education is one of the most neglected areas in home schooling. Too often we simply send our children out to ride their bikes or play hopscotch, giving them little or no instruction or supervision. We parents frequently have no specific goals in mind when it comes to physical education, other than getting a little free time for ourselves. Granted, we all need some free time as home-schooling parents, but our children need a proper physical education program, too.

Home schoolers seem to have an abundant choice of curricula in every subject area, except physical education. Again and again I hear the question, "What can we do for gym class?" Yet, there just isn't much available to give us any answers. We try to recall what we did back in the old days when we were in school, but a school-based physical education program just doesn't seem to fit the home-school situation, especially when we wish to maintain Biblical principles in all of our activities.

The reason for this manual is to give purpose and direction to the physical education program, to set goals, and to give some practical ways for home schoolers to reach those goals, in keeping with Biblical principles. Let's give our children a complete education, neglecting nothing, yet keeping all things in their proper perspective.

Alexander D. Marini

Acknowledgements

A few Scripture quotations are taken from the New American Standard Version of the Bible, © 1960, 1962, 1963, 1968, 1971, 1972,1973, 1975, 1977 by the Lockman Foundation. Used by permission and indicated with (NASV).

All other Scripture quotations are taken from the King James Version of the Bible. All non-Bible quotations have been used with written permission from the publishers where required. Studies cited in Chapter 2 are included with special permission granted by *Current Health 2*, published by Weekly Reader Corporation. Copyright © 1991 by Weekly Reader Corporation.

Many of the exercises, games and activities in this manual are versions that I developed in my years of teaching physical education; I took none of them from any published work. However, my teachers, colleagues, friends and students have shared a number of the exercises, games and activities that are included, so I have no way of knowing who originally invented them. This leaves me unable to ask permission and give proper acknowledgement to the originators. If any reader of this manual should be aware of the originators of any of these exercises, games or activities, I would appreciate being informed so that I might follow proper procedure in giving credit where credit is due.

Finally, I wish to give special thanks to my wife, Susan, and fellow teacher, Ed Kane, for their many suggestions and for proofreading the manuscript to make it readable and usable.

How To Use This Manual

Undoubtedly, you're in a hurry to get your program rolling, so you may be tempted to flip right to the Activities section of the manual and skip all the philosophizing at the beginning. Please don't do that. Most likely, the whole approach to physical education being presented in this manual is markedly different from anything you've ever heard, read or experienced. The Philosophy and Preparation parts of the manual set the stage for all the rest.

The manual is self-explanatory if you start reading from the beginning and read the introductory parts of each section before going on to the activities. Don't worry, you won't have to read the whole manual to get your program going, but you do need to read the Philosophy and Preparation parts first, as they will lay the necessary groundwork for building your program. If you skip them, it may be difficult to understand and effectively use the activities, since the activities are an outgrowth of the philosophy. So set aside a couple of hours tonight, and take a fresh look at what physical education is all about.

PART I

PHILOSOPHY

CHAPTER 1

A BIBLICAL BASIS

PHYSICAL EDUCATION IN PERSPECTIVE

"For bodily exercise profiteth little...." (1 Tim. 4:8)

How's that for openers in a physical education manual? You probably thought I was going to try to convince you that physical education was the most important thing in the world. Well, from God's perspective, it isn't. As Christians, we must see things from God's perspective and view them as He does. But before we jump to a hasty conclusion about this verse and cut physical education from the program, let's consider the context of this statement. In reading the whole chapter, we find Paul exhorting Timothy to "exercise" himself "unto godliness," as he states in the remainder of verse 8:

> "...but godliness is profitable unto all things, having promise of the life that now is, and of that which is to come." (1 Tim. 4:8)

Paul's point here is not to condemn bodily exercise, but to put it in its proper place. When compared to the spiritual disciplines, bodily exercise truly is of "little profit." The exercise of prayer and meditation, Bible study, devotion to good works, fellowship, ministries and general obedience to God's commands are all much more important than bodily exercise. These are profitable both for the present life, and the life to come. Therefore, spiritual disciplines must be our highest priorities. However, that doesn't mean that bodily exercise is wrong or totally unprofitable. Hopefully, we all brush our teeth, try to eat right, get sufficient rest, bathe and practice a host of other good health habits, simply because the inevitable will happen if we don't. Good health habits have no "direct" eternal value, so, in that sense, they all "profit little," but they *are* necessary for this life. This is the

Biblical perspective of "bodily exercise," so let it be our perspective as well. Be assured, physical education does have its place in a Christian home-school program, but we need to be careful to keep it in its place.

Although the Bible does not make a lot of direct statements about physical education, there are a number of principles mentioned in the Bible that can be applied to the subject. Admittedly, the passages to be cited will not be in the context of specifically addressing the issue of physical education, but when the Bible does not specifically address a matter, we have no alternative but to apply general principles in a reasonable way. Let's consider a few of these principles to establish a Biblical basis for including physical education in the Christian home-school program.

The Need for Physical Activity. The human body was designed from the beginning to be physically active. Even before the fall, Adam was commissioned by God "to dress" the Garden of Eden, "and to keep it" (Gen 2:15). "Dressing" and "keeping" the garden surely involved physical labor, and in those days, it was without the aid of labor-saving devices. After the fall, that physical labor was intensified to be hard, toilsome labor, as a result of the curse:

> "In the sweat of thy face shalt thou eat bread...."
> (Gen. 3:19)

Man has since invented many labor-saving devices, so that most of us no longer have to "sweat" in order to produce bread. Most Americans live a sedentary lifestyle with little or no physical activity. Although such a lifestyle does not violate any of God's commandments, it is contrary to God's design for human life. Our bodies were made to be active, and the more we avoid physical activity, the more our physical health degenerates. Lack of physical exercise has been identified as a risk factor in most of the major health problems of our day. On the other hand, regular and proper physical exercise has been demonstrated to significantly contribute to overall health and longevity.

If we did all our chores the old way, and spent most of our working hours involved in a wide variety of hard physical-labor activities, then our fitness needs would be well met. But such a life style is quite impractical for most of us in this day and age (if not impossible); therefore, physical education is essential to a balanced educational program for children, as well as adults.

The Value of Human Life. Human life is very special to God because "God created man in His own image" (Gen. 1:27). He commands us not to kill (Gen. 9:6), hate (1 Jn. 4:20), or even to curse men (Jas. 3:9), all for the same that men bear God's image. God dwells in our physical bodies as His New Testament temple (1 Cor. 3:16). He commands us not to defile or destroy His temple (1 Cor. 3:17), and indicates that it is wrong to sin against one's own body (1 Cor. 6:18-20). Since God made us, He also owns us and has all rights over us:

"...ye are not your own...ye are bought with a price;
therefore glorify God in your body, and in your spirit, which are God's."
(1 Cor. 6:19-20)

Human life, including the physical body, is therefore sacred and deserves utmost respect and proper care.

Temple Maintenance. The temple of the Old Testament was God's dwelling place. In 1 Chronicles 26:27, we read that money was set aside for the maintenance of the temple. Someone also had to devote time and energy performing the upkeep of the temple, lest it fall into disrepair. Nothing in this life lasts long or functions effectively, unless it is maintained. Your body, the New Testament temple, is where God dwells today. Like the Old Testament temple, your body must also be maintained. We need to set aside time, energy and money to perform the upkeep required to keep these temples in proper condition. If we don't, the inevitable will happen.

"By much slothfulness the building decayeth."
(Ecc. 10:18)

Health and God's Will. God reserves the right to afflict our health for certain purposes, such as chastening for sin (1 Cor 11:26-32) or to prevent us from sin (2 Cor. 12:7-12). God may also allow Satan to afflict our health for reasons that He may not explain (Job 2:6-7).

There may also be times when God asks us to lay down our health, and even our lives, as a sacrifice for others or as a testimony of our faith (Lk. 14:26-27). Yet, in general, it is God's will for us to be healthy, as John says:

"Beloved, I wish above all things that thou mayest prosper
and be in health, even as thy soul prospereth."
(3 Jn. 2)

Paul states:

"No man ever hated his own flesh, but nourisheth and cherisheth it...."
(Eph. 5:29)

We must conclude from all this that it is good and proper in the sight of God to do those things that promote good health and to abstain from those things that do not. Therefore, physical education is a worthy and valuable part of a balanced lifestyle and must be included in a complete educational program.

CHAPTER 2

GOALS

The Focal Point. Physical Education was first introduced into the American school system because it was observed that those who were physically active performed better academically. Therefore, physical fitness was the focal point of physical education activities. Today, however, athletic competition is usually the focal point of physical education activities. Because of this, we often get carried away with sports to the point of neglecting physical fitness, jeopardizing our health and risking injuries. We also demonstrate poor stewardship of our time and energy as we become all-consumed with endless practice, trying to be "number one."

A further concern is that present day physical education programs are failing to accomplish their primary purpose. Physical Education is supposed to provide proper physical activity to maintain God's temple, but the following studies clearly indicate that recent programs are ineffective.

"A 1989 study by the Amateur Athletic Union found that 68 percent of 9 million Americans between the ages of six and seventeen couldn't pass tests for strength, endurance, and flexibility. The research also documented a steady decline in fitness in this age group between 1980 and 1989. The number of students who scored "satisfactory" on the tests declined from 43 percent in 1980 to 32 percent in 1989.

In another study, the U.S. Department of Health and Human Services compared school-age children of today with those of twenty years ago. Researchers found that today's children have a higher percentage of body fat than children of twenty years ago. A study reported in the *American Journal of Diseases of Children* found that during the last fifteen years, obesity in six- to eleven-year-old children went up 54 percent and increased 39 percent in children aged twelve to seventeen" (Kamberg, 5-6). Granted, numerous factors have contributed to the decline in fitness levels: sedentary entertainment, labor saving devices, and cultural and dietary changes. But whatever the cause, the fact remains that today's physical education programs are not meeting the fitness needs of our young people.

For all the time, energy, money, equipment, facilities, technology and publicity that go into our "sports-oriented" physical education programs today, it's plain to see that our focus has been on the wrong thing: namely, sports, instead of physical fitness. The elite chosen few continually improve their athletic performance, but it is at the expense of the masses, whose fitness levels continually decline. Sports, you see, are not designed for fitness; they are designed for competition. That's why athletic teams on virtually every level of competition employ fitness programs in their training; playing the sport itself does not maintain fitness.

Although many physical education activities can be fun and "mildly" competitive, we must not let this be our focal point. Rather, our focal point must be the maintenance and refreshment of God's temple, keeping fun, competition and sports in their proper place. For this reason, "physical fitness" will be presented as the core of the physical education program in this manual.

Overall Aim. In general, the purpose of Christian education is to prepare children for a life that will bring glory to God. Such preparation involves all aspects of our being, both physical and non-physical. In order for growth and development to take place in both realms, we need nurture, care, discipline, challenge and exercise. Thus, physical education is a necessary part of a balanced educational program.

The overall aim of physical education is not to produce professional athletes, nor is it to keep our children entertained with fun activities during their school years; neither is our purpose to simply meet state requirements or develop attractive physiques. Rather, our aim in physical education is *maintenance and refreshment of God's temple:* to provide all that is necessary to maintain and promote the growth, development and soundness of the physical body, which is the temple of the Holy Spirit. In so doing, we contribute greatly to the general well-being of the whole person. This enhances all pursuits of life, expands our capabilities, and helps us to achieve our maximum potential as human beings in reflecting the character and nature of God, which is His purpose in creating us.

GENERAL GOALS

1. To gain a respect and appreciation for the human body as being God's "fearfully and wonderfully made" temple

2. To develop and maintain a good level of physical fitness through following a balanced fitness program

3. To learn and develop work and recreational skills

4. To learn to enjoy the discipline of physical activity

5. To develop good health habits that can be carried on throughout life

6. To learn proper attitudes in working and playing with others

CHAPTER 3

PHILOSOPHY OF GAMES

Recreational Games. Recreational games are an important part of the Christian home-school physical education program. They provide wholesome exercise, fun, and family togetherness, and they help with stress management. The word *recreation* is defined as "refreshment of body or mind" (Funk and Wagnalls).

Everyone needs refreshment, and we will all seek it in one form or another, so recreational games are one good way to be refreshed. However, in order to be truly "recreational," games must be either non-competitive or very mildly competitive. We must make sure that everyone vigorously participates in the game and enjoys it. In recreational games we should play hard, but we can laugh about our mistakes, and no one really cares who wins. We have no leagues, no set teams, no first string, no bench warmers, no championships, no trophies, and even the rules are rearranged to suit our particular needs, goals, and the limitations of our abilities and facilities. If the game doesn't refresh us physically and mentally, then it isn't "recreational."

Competitive Athletics. Some home schoolers involve their children in competitive athletic leagues such as YMCA, church or community leagues, or school leagues. There is also a movement today to develop competitive athletic teams and leagues specifically for home schoolers. The feeling seems to be that our children might miss out on something important if they are deprived of the opportunity to participate in competitive athletics. Perhaps we need to reconsider the matter. I've spent much of my life involved in most of the above-mentioned competitive athletic leagues, as well as during my three-year military experience. Short of my work in prison ministry, I have yet to find a place on earth where human depravity is manifest more openly than the athletic locker room. The filthy language, the jokes, the fights, the degrading behavior—I'll spare you the gory details, but please permit me to cite one study that exposes just a few of the far-reaching effects of participation in competitive athletics:

A study by Dr. James Puffer, an adjunct associate professor and chief of the division of family medicine at the UCLA School of Medicine, found that student-athletes are one and a half times more likely than non-athletes to have greater number of sexual partners and. . .have a four-fold greater frequency of sexually transmitted diseases than non-athletes, according to the study (*On Target Magazine* / January 1993, p.2).

We Christian parents really ought to consider the wisdom of sending our children "out to play" with such. Scripture warns, "bad company corrupts good morals" (1 Cor. 15:3e NASV). We are further commanded, "I wrote unto you in an epistle not to company with fornicators" (1 Cor. 5:9).

It is no secret that competitive athletes are notorious for immorality. Present day super stars openly boast of their promiscuity. But beyond all that, the very nature of competition needs to be examined from a Biblical perspective.

The dictionary defines *competition* as follows:

> "contention of two or more for the same object or for superiority;
> rivalry, or contending emulously (enviously or with jealousy)."
> (Funk and Wagnalls)

Does such a description fit any of our goals as Christian home schoolers? We've all seen enough of athletic competition to know that attitudes of pride, win at all cost, rivalry, hostility, and even hatred are commonly seen at many competitive athletic events, even those of Christian schools and churches.

In contrast to recreational games, which tend to refresh us physically and mentally, competitive athletics often require us to push ourselves to exhaustion. Recreational games tend to relieve stress, while competitive athletics tend to be an additional source of stress in our already stress-filled lives. Many professional athletes are involved in drug abuse in an effort to cope with the stress of their profession.

Further, when we consider the time, energy and money that typically goes into competitive athletics, it becomes rather difficult to justify it with all that the Bible has to say about "stewardship." The primary striving of a Christian is to be for spiritual progress, not athletic success. Whenever the Bible specifically mentions competitive athletics, it is always for the purpose of illustrating the whole-hearted pursuit of spiritual things:

> "I press toward the mark for the prize of the high
> calling of God in Christ Jesus"
> (Phil. 3:14).

"Wherefore, seeing we also are compassed about with so
great a cloud of witnesses, let us lay aside every
weight, and the sin which doth so easily beset us, and
let us run with patience the race that is set before us."
(Heb. 12:1)

I have fought the good fight, I have finished my course, I
have kept the faith: Henceforth there is laid up for me a
crown of righteousness, which the Lord, the righteous
judge, shall give me at that day: and not to me only, but
unto all them also that love his appearing."
(2 Tim. 4:7)

Such illustrations are not used to encourage Christians to pursue athletic success, but rather to pursue spiritual things with the same vigor and all-out commitment as the athlete. Indeed, to give ourselves to athletic pursuits would defeat the very purpose of these exhortations, for "no man can
serve two masters: for either he will hate the one, and love the other; or else he will hold to the one,
and despise the other. Ye cannot serve God and mammon" (Mt. 6:24). Consider Paul's words:

"And every man that striveth for the mastery is temperate in all things.
Now *they* do it to obtain a corruptible crown; but *we* an incorruptible." (italics added)
(1 Cor. 9:25)

Now who are *they*? *They* are unbelievers, who have nothing to strive for except the corruptible rewards
of this world. But <u>we</u> are the children of God and are to strive for the incorruptible. This is not to suggest that all those who compete are unbelievers, nor that our salvation hangs on this issue. Our salvation rests in our faith in the shed blood of Christ, and nothing more. I am personally acquainted with
many well-meaning Christians who are involved in competitive athletics, and I did so myself for much
of my own Christian experience. But let us consider our calling, brethren, and take a fresh look at this
issue that has gone virtually unchallenged by the church for half a century.

A study of church history will reveal that it wasn't until the mid 1900s that the church opened its
arms to sports, shortly after sports became popular in secular American society. Throughout the cen-
turies, nearly every major denomination condemned sports in an effort to keep the saints "unspotted
by the world." The early church fathers, such as Tatian, Tertullian and Clement, denounced the
games of their day because of the immodesty, brutality and idolatry associated with them.

We must admit that things haven't changed much, and immodesty, brutality and idolatry are still
typically associated with sports. In our present society sport stars are idolized, and athletic success is
coveted to the point of idolatry (Col. 3:5). In a lecture called "Steroids in Strength Training,"

Dr. James Lynch, team physician for Penn State University, cited a poll that was taken of Olympic athletes. The Olympians were asked the following question:

"If you could take a pill that would guarantee that you would win a gold medal, but would probably cause your death 10 years from now, would you take it?"

The *majority* of Olympic athletes answered *"yes."*

Let us consider whether competitive athletics really lines up with the foundational goals of our physical education program, and our general goals as Christian home schoolers. It's one thing for a family to play a backyard game now and then, or to get together occasionally for a support group recreation day; it's quite another to become involved in competitive athletics. It is the author's opinion that such involvement will not contribute to our spiritual growth, nor is it a necessary part of the physical education program. Our program can be balanced and complete without competitive athletics.

The Nature of Games. Games don't have to be "competitive" to be vigorous, refreshing and fun. Many games can actually be "cooperative" in nature, rather than competitive. Please bear with me as we consider a few principles that the Bible presents for Christian attitudes and behavior concerning the principles of <u>competition</u> versus <u>cooperation</u>. Admittedly, the contexts of the following passages are not directly addressing the matter of games, but principles are principles, none-the-less.

> "...but they measuring themselves by themselves,
> and comparing themselves among themselves, are not wise."
> (2 Corinthians 10:12)

Is a competitive athletic contest anything other than two people or teams comparing themselves among themselves? God says this is not wise. He further warns about comparisons:

> "...that no one of you be puffed up for one against another.
> For who maketh thee to differ from another?
> and what hast thou that thou didst not receive?"
> (1 Corinthians 4:6-7)

The self-glorification that is the prime motivator for athletic success, we must admit, is directly against Scripture.

> "Then there arose a reasoning among them [Jesus' disciples],
> which of them should be greatest."
> (Luke 9:46)

To this, Jesus responded:

"...he that is least among you all, the same shall be great."
(Luke 9:48)

Is a competitive athletic contest anything other than two people or teams trying to demonstrate which is greatest? Jesus says that this is not the way to attain greatness. The preacher of Ecclesiastes agrees:

"And I have seen that every labor and every skill
which is done is the result of rivalry between a man
and his neighbor. This too is vanity and striving after wind."
(Ecc. 4:4 NASV)

Consider further that competition, by nature, requires one person or team to "beat" another; often, the only way to win is by causing the opposition to lose. In competition, my success is dependent upon your failure; I can't win unless I make you lose.

On the other hand, we are frequently exhorted in Scripture to cooperate with one another; to strive together in a unified effort to accomplish God's purposes.

"So we, being many, are one body in Christ, and every one members one of another."
(Rom. 12:5)

"Endeavoring to keep the unity of the Spirit in the bond of peace. There is one body...."
(Eph. 4:3-4)

"...the whole body fitly joined together and compacted by that which every joint supplieth,
according to the effectual working in the measure of every part,
maketh increase of the body unto the edifying of itself in love."
(Eph. 4:16)

"...stand fast in one spirit, with one mind striving together for the faith of the gospel."
(Phil. 1:27)

It is rather difficult to reconcile competition with these Biblical principles. Cooperation, on the other hand, fits quite well. Why throw all these principles away just because it's time for gym class? How much better to use gym class to reinforce these principles, instead of contradicting them. Isn't there enough unavoidable sibling rivalry between your children without fostering it?

It is the author's opinion that games that are cooperative in nature are to be preferred over games that are competitive in nature, as this is far more fitting for Christians. Whenever possible, the games presented in this manual have been restructured to be cooperative in nature, or the competitive element has been reduced or removed. For those who would like a greater selection of non-competitive games, check your local library for *Non-Competitive Games*, by Susan Butler, or *The Cooperative Sports & Games Book*, by Terry Orlick. If you wish to purchase these books, you can write to the publishers, whose addresses are given in the bibliography.

Modifying Game Rules. There's no need to play games by "big league" rules. Often, younger players will enjoy and benefit much more from a game if the rules are modified. Most games can be played either indoors or outdoors, with big groups or small, and with older or younger children, if the rules are sufficiently modified. Don't be afraid to change the rules to suit your facilities, equipment, the ability level of your children and the goals of your program. It's even OK to have different rules for different individual players, depending on their skill level. Experiment with different versions until you develop games that provide refreshment for everyone. And keep the rules to a minimum; use only enough rules to have a safe, vigorous game. Usually, the more rules we have, the more interruptions there are in the game, which greatly reduces the fitness benefits of the game. For this reason some games in this manual have been restructured to avoid interruptions and increase the amount of activity in the game.

Reducing Competitiveness. Some games, such as baseball, are difficult to change from competitive to cooperative, and scoring points becomes inevitable, since that is the object of the game. But usually we can still play these games if we make some efforts to reduce the competitive spirit. One way to do this is to avoid keeping track of the score. Score keeping is not only a nuisance to the teacher, but a source of discouragement or pride to the players. Score keeping tends to intensify the competitive spirit and adds stress to the game. For these reasons, I suggest that we avoid keeping track of the score altogether. Since the game is for fun, exercise and refreshment, anyway, it doesn't really matter who has more points at the end. Just play your best and forget the score. If we all have a good workout and are refreshed by the game, then we all win. Another option is to switch the teams around every few minutes during the game so that no one remains on the same team for very long.

Children who have grown up with set teams and keeping score may not like these changes at first, but they usually agree with them after a while. Each time they hint about keeping score, take the opportunity to remind them that the game is just for refreshment and exercise. If wrong attitudes persist, it may be best to replace the game with one that is more cooperative in nature.

Elimination Games. There are some games that eliminate players, such as musical chairs. It is usually the same child that gets eliminated first, and he always ends up losing and feeling discouraged. To make matters worse, the child who always gets eliminated first is the one who needs more experience in the game, but he never gets it because he is always sitting out. Rather than eliminating players, it is wiser to eliminate those kinds of games, or else change the game so that no one gets eliminated. Let's make sure that *everyone* has a positive experience in physical education class.

PART II

PREPARATION

CHAPTER 4

PLANNING YOUR PROGRAM

THE PRINCIPLE OF BALANCE

Balance is a fundamental principle that is necessary to sustain all life. We can see balance everywhere in God's creation. A balanced lifestyle is the key to good health, both in the physical and non-physical realms of a human being. If we maintain balance in both realms, it will all work together for the general well-being of an individual.

For spiritual health, we need a balance of prayer and meditation, Bible study, Christian fellowship and Christian service. If any of these areas is over-emphasized to the exclusion of another, our spiritual health and development will be less than it could be.

For physical health, we need balance in nutrition, sleep and waking time, and rest and activity. Any imbalances here will lead to all sorts of health problems. And when it comes to physical education, we also need balance. A well-rounded physical education program will include each of the following areas, which will be discussed at length in later sections of the manual.

PHYSICAL FITNESS

This is the core of physical education. A balanced physical fitness program includes flexibility, strength and aerobic exercises.

SKILLS

These are the individual parts that make up activities: running, jumping, throwing, catching, etc. Work skills and recreational skills must be reviewed and practiced, and new ones learned.

ACTIVITIES

This is where we put our skills together to perform a complex activity. Work activities and recreational activities must be reviewed and practiced, and new ones learned.

RESEARCH PROJECTS.

To gain an appreciation for the wonders of God's temple (your body), it's a good idea to do a physical education research project now and then. Research projects are not a mandatory part of physical education, but can be a very profitable extra. Design the projects to help the child understand how his body works and what's happening in his body as he works and does exercises. Use resource books from the library, encyclopedias, or the child's own science books. A few suggested projects are given at the end of each of the physical fitness sections of the manual.

All of the above need not be included in every physical education class, but each should be included on a regular basis.

PLANNING THE YEAR

Planning your physical education program involves several steps. Some *forms* have been included at the end of this section to help in your planning. There are also *samples* of the forms already filled out, to give you an idea of how to do this. You are free to make copies of the forms for your own personal use, if you wish to use them. These forms are not only handy for planning, but they also provide a documented record.

When planning, keep in mind that both work and play have their place in every person's life, and they need to be kept in balance; too much of either is unhealthy. It is to be hoped that as children grow older, they will spend more time working and less time playing.

Before getting too involved in planning, it would be wise to flip through the rest of the manual to familiarize yourself with the specific activities that are covered. Some activities can only be done outdoors, so it would be wise to select indoor units for the winter months. The following units work well indoors:

Basic Ball Skills	Gymnastics	Hand/Eye Coordination	Handball
Locomotor Skills	Paddleball/Racquetball	Pillow Polo	Ping Pong

SETTING OBJECTIVES

The first step in planning your physical education program for the year is to set goals and objectives. The general goals given in the Goals section of the manual provide some general direction, but you will have to add specific objectives to these. Make a list of the specific activities you want your child to participate in this year in physical education. At the end of this section, there is a sample of objectives to give you an idea of what they are all about, as well as a reproducible form for your own use. Go ahead and make at least one copy of the Objectives form and fill it in now with your objectives for this year.

Note. While listing your objectives, it's a good idea to refer back to your general goals to be sure that your objectives are in line with them.

UNIT PLANS

A "unit" (in physical education) is a period of time in which we study and practice a particular activity, and learn and improve the skills related to it. Once you have listed your yearly objectives, the next step is to break the year up into units; perhaps 12, 15, or even 18 units for the year. A unit could be as short or long as you want, but would usually cover a period of about three weeks. At the end of this section you will find a sample of Unit Plans and a reproducible form for organizing your own unit plans for the year. Go ahead and make at least one copy of the Unit Plans form and fill it in now.

To fill out the form, simply set the dates for each unit and fill in the specific activities you plan to cover during each unit. You do not need to include specific details here about the activities; it's just a form for planning when you will do each different activity.

Note. While planning your units, it's a good idea to refer back to your general goals and objectives to be sure that your units are aimed at reaching these goals and objectives.

You might consider continuing your physical fitness program throughout the year, without taking the summer off. We don't stop eating balanced meals or practicing dental care just because it's summer vacation. Neither should we discontinue our fitness program; it is a necessary part of a healthy life style.

For further details about Activity Units, see Chapter 12.

DAILY LESSON PLANS

The last step in planning is to decide which specific activities you will cover on each day of a unit. At this point you will have to decide how often to have physical education class. We are free to have it as often as we want, and we can get by with as little as two or three sessions a week in order to simply maintain physical fitness. But for a good balance in the daily life, you might consider having physical education every school day. This gives us a chance to participate in a variety of work and recreational activities from day to day, and provides a much needed break from academics at that time of day when your children can no longer sit still. You might consider arranging your weekly schedule something like this: Monday, Wednesday and Friday do physical fitness and game activities; Tuesday, Thursday and Saturday do work activities. This is just a suggestion, and you can arrange it any way you like, but it is good to have some physical activity every day.

At the end of this section you will find a sample of Daily Lesson Plans to give you an idea of what they are about. There is also a reproducible form to use for your own daily lesson plans. The form is lengthy enough to plan daily lessons for a three-week unit, even if you have physical education six days a week. You will need a separate copy of the Daily Lesson Plan form for each unit you cover during the year. Go ahead and make at least one copy of the form now, and fill it in for your first unit.

The form is set up from left to right in the order that you will carry out each part of a physical education class. To use the form in planning your daily lessons, simply fill in the dates that you will have physical education during that period of time. Then fill in the fitness activities, spacing them appropriately from day to day (see the Physical Fitness section of the manual for further details on how frequently to perform fitness activities).

Next, skip over to the "activity" column and fill in the specific activities that you will do on each specific day. Then go back to the "skills" column and fill in the specific skills that need to be reviewed or learned in order to perform the activity.

For the units in which you decide to do research projects, it's good to assign one project to a unit. Divide the project up into several parts, and spread it out over the unit, filling in the specific part of the project to be done each day.

Note. You've probably noticed that things don't always go according to our plans, and we often get different ideas as time progresses; so don't be afraid to alter your general goals, objectives, unit plans and daily plans as you see the need.

LESSON PROCEDURE

The following are seven steps that I recommend in carrying out one lesson in physical education:

1. Introduction - Explain what you will be doing today in gym class.

2. Warm-up - Walk briskly or jog for one to two minutes; then perform the flexibility exercise routine.

3. Exercise - Perform whatever strength and/or aerobic exercises are planned for the day.

4. Review - Briefly quiz the children on the skills that have been covered so far in the unit. Practice some if necessary.

5. Instruction - Explain, demonstrate and practice any new skills, always emphasizing safety and proper technique.

6. Activity - Perform whatever activity is planned.

7. Cool-down - Walk one to two minutes and perform the flexibility exercise routine.

INDIVIDUAL DIFFERENCES

One last thing to consider when planning is the individual differences of children. In a conventional school system children are usually grouped according to age, and they are all required to perform the same exercises for the same number of repetitions. They are also required to perform the same skills and to compete against one another. The "average child" becomes the standard by which all others are measured. This is far from ideal and usually produces pride in those who excel, and utter discouragement in those who don't. There is a much better way.

God has made each of us different in many respects, and no two people grow up in exactly the same environment. God gives us different levels of potential in different areas, and we develop at different rates. Because of this, home schoolers have a great advantage over conventional systems, as we can tailor our programs for our individual children to a much greater degree. We don't have to make separate unit and lesson plans for each child, but we do need to make allowances and modifications for each one.

As various exercises, skills, and activities are presented throughout this manual, please keep in mind the individual differences that exist in your children. Don't expect them to perform with equal ability, nor to learn new things equally fast. And above all, don't compare your children with one another. You'll need to continually remind them (and yourself) that God has made each of us unique. The key to individualizing activities is to meet each child at his *present* level of ability in each specific activity. Age and body size make no difference. And just because someone does well at one activity, that doesn't necessarily mean he will do well at another. As a general rule, modify the activity enough so that each child can *successfully* accomplish whatever is being required of him. Then challenge him with something a little more difficult than he has done before.

If these principles are followed, children will develop a positive attitude toward physical education activities, and we can do a much more thorough job at providing all that is needed for their growth and development.

GRADING

Grading is not usually required for home schoolers, but for those who wish to give grades on a periodic basis, here are four categories upon which to base a grade.

Effort - This is a subjective grade and should reflect how vigorously (in your opinion) the child participates in physical education class.

Fitness - This is not based on comparing the child with others, seeing how fast he can do a set number of repetitions. Instead, grade him on whether he properly performs the exercises you taught him, and whether he actually does all the fitness work you require of him on a daily basis.

Skills - Grade the child on how well he learns and performs the skills you taught him, focusing on the technique. You might subtract points for improper positioning of arms, legs, hands, feet, etc. You can also grade on successful performance of skills, such as in basketball, seeing how many baskets he shoots out of ten shots, or if he's able to dribble the length of the court.

Research Projects - Grade the child on his written assignments, models, etc.

If you choose to do testing and grading, it is wise to tell the child that he will be given a formal test on fitness and skills, as this will help him to pay attention to detail when things are presented. It works well to let each category carry 25 percent of the grade.

FORMS

The following are sample forms to facilitate the organization of your physical education program.

_____

School Year

PHYSICAL EDUCATION OBJECTIVES

Physical Fitness

_____
_____
_____
_____
_____

Work Activities

_____
_____
_____
_____
_____

Recreational Activities

_____
_____
_____
_____
_____

Research Projects

_____
_____
_____
_____
_____

1994/1995
School Year

PHYSICAL EDUCATION OBJECTIVES

Physical Fitness

Review and practice exercises for physical strength, flexibility and cardiovascular endurance.

Work Activities

Review and practice skills in lawn care, gardening, snow removal and firewood preparation.

Review and practice proper attitudes for working with others.

Recreational Activities

Review and practice old and new simple games.

Review and practice proper attitudes for playing with others.

Review and practice swimming skills and water safety.

Review and practice bike safety.

Research Projects

Improve understanding of various body systems.

UNIT PLANS

UNIT #	DATES	FITNESS			ACTIVITIES		RESEARCH
		Flexibility	Strength	Aerobics	Work	Recreation	Projects
1							
2							
3							
4							
5							
6							
7							
8							
9							
10							
11							
12							
13							
14							
15							
16							
17							

1995/96

UNIT PLANS

UNIT #	DATES	FITNESS			ACTIVITIES		RESEARCH
		Flexibility	Strength	Aerobics	Work	Recreation	Projects
1	9/2 to 9/21	Beginner Routine	Beginner Routine	Run Bike	Garden Firewood Lawn Care	Flag Football	Skeleton
2	9/23 to 10/12	"	"	"	"	Bike Safety	
3	10/14 to 11/2	"	"	"	"	Tether Ball	
4	11/4 to 11/23	"	Add 2 exercises	"	"	Socccer	CV System
5	11/25 to 12/14	"	"	"	"	Basic Ball Skills	
6	12/16 to 1/4	"	"	Jump Rope Mini Trampoline	Snow Removal Firewood	Gymnastics	
7	1/6 to 1/25	"	"	Sledding Skating	"	Pillow Polo	Respiratory System
8	1/27 to 2/15	"	"	"	"	Trampoline Stunts	
9	2/17 to 3/7	"	"	"	"	Basket-Ball	
10	3/9 to 3/28	"	"	Run Bike	"	Paddle Ball	Muscles
11	3/30 to 4/18	"	"	"	Garden Lawn Care Firewood	Chase Games	
12	4/20 to 5/9	"	"	Roller Skating	"	Flag Football	
13	5/11 to 5/30	"	"	"	"	Base-Ball	Nerves
14	6/1 to 6/20	"	"	Swim Run Bike	"	Water Safety Baseball	
15	6/22 to 7/11	"	"	"	"	Swim Badminton	
16	7/13 to 8/1	"	"	"	"	Swim Frisbee	Blood
17	8/3 to 8/22	"	"	"	"	Swim	
18	8/24 to 9/1	"	"	"	"	Locomotor Skills	

DAILY LESSON PLANS FOR UNIT #_____

DATES	FITNESS			SKILLS	ACTIVITIES	RESEARCH
	Flexibility	Strength	Aerobics			

DAILY LESSON PLANS FOR UNIT # *1*

DATES	FITNESS			SKILLS	ACTIVITIES	RESEARCH
	Flexibility	Strength	Aerobics			
9/2/96	*Beginner Routine 15 Seconds*	*Beginner Routine 10 Repetitions*		*Demo: Starting: oil, gas, throttle, watch feet*	*Mow Lawn*	*Draw Upper Skeleton*
9/3/96			*Run 4 Minutes*	*Demo: Rake use for leaves/thatch*	*Rake Lawn*	
9/4/96	"	"		*Demo: Overhand throw, catch practice 10 times*	*Flag Football for 2 players*	
9/5/96			*Bike 15 Minutes*	*Demo: Save space prevent fall ride on right*	*Stack Firewood*	
9/6/96	"	"		*Review: throw/catch practice 10 times*	*Flag Football for 2 players*	
9/7/96			*Run 4 Minutes*	*Demo: Use of spade fork*	*Dig Potatoes*	
9/9/96	"	"		*Demo: Punt practice 10 times*	*Flag Football for 3 players*	
9/10/96			*Bike 15 Minutes*	*Demo: Hand signals right/left turn practice 10 times*		*Draw Lower Skeleton*
9/11/96	"	"		*Review Punt practice 10 times*	*Flag Football for 3 players*	
9/12/96			*Run 4 Minutes*			
9/13/96	"	"			*Stack Firewood*	
9/14/96			*Bike 15 Minutes*	*Review: Right/left Demo: Stop signal practice 10 times*	*Dig Potatoes*	*Color Skeleton*
9/16/96	"	"		*Review: Starting Demo: Diagonal mowing pattern*	*Mow Lawn*	
9/17/96			*Run 4 Minutes*		*Rake Lawn*	
9/18/96	"	"		*Demo: Place-kick practice 10 times*	*Flag Football for 3 players*	
9/19/96			*Bike 15 Minutes*		*Stack Firewood*	
9/20/96	"	"		*Review: Place-kick practice times*	*Flag Football for 3 players*	*Make Clay Skeleton*

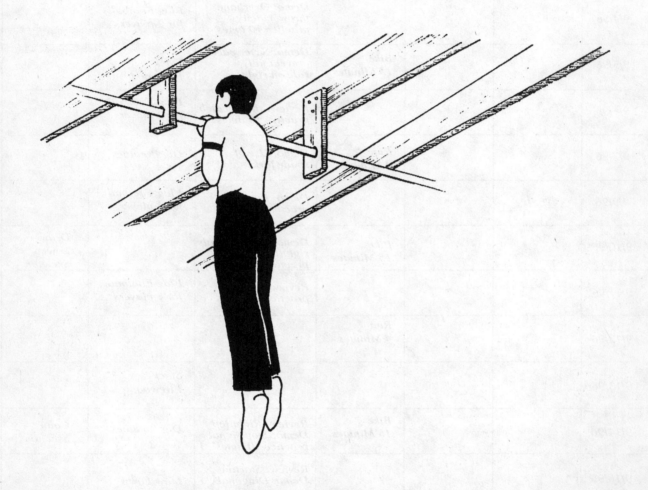

CHAPTER 5

EQUIPMENT

Gymnasiums and big athletic fields are nice extras, but they do not make or break a physical education program. Special items, such as stationary bikes, rowing machines, weights, treadmills, etc., are also unnecessary. These things can contribute to physical fitness if used regularly, but they usually become ornaments in most homes due to lack of use.

There are many so-called "exercise machines" on the market that *supposedly* do the work for you: vibrating belts, flab rollers, massage chairs and benches, etc. They promise weight loss and fitness without effort. Although these machines may provide a source of entertainment (watching the flab shake and roll), they are virtually worthless as far as physical fitness is concerned, and they do little or nothing to maintain the "temple."

With some basic, inexpensive equipment, a number of common household items, and a little creativity, we can do a good job of achieving the goals of our physical education program. The items needed for each activity will be mentioned in the section describing the activity.

Purchasing Equipment. Some physical education items can be purchased at local department stores or sporting goods stores, but they don't always carry everything we'd like to have. For items that you can't find locally, you might want to order a catalog from a physical education equipment supplier. The supplier listed below is one of the most reasonably priced that I have found, and they carry a wide variety of equipment. They will send you a free catalog if you call or write for it.

Flaghouse Inc.
150 No. Macqueston Pkwy.
Mt. Vernon, N.Y. 10550
(914) 699-1900
Fax # 914 699 2961

Homemade Equipment. For those who are handy at making things, I encourage home-made equipment whenever possible. Get your children involved in the construction if they're old enough, but be careful that the equipment you make is safe; test it out yourself. For each activity in the manual, if an item can be homemade, a description is given for its construction.

Clothing. We don't need special uniforms for physical education. Our clothing should be loose, to allow free movement, and modest, to obey God's command in 1 Tim. 2:9-10. God expects His people to dress modestly all the time, and gym class is no exception. We have all grown up in a society in which no one questions immodest dress, especially for athletic activities. Today it's just expected that joggers wear tank tops and skimpy shorts, and swimmers wear next to nothing.

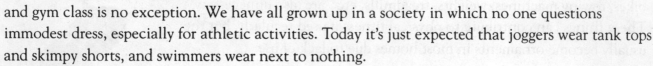

We must remember that immodesty and immorality go hand in hand; that's why both are so prevalent in our society. Rom. 14:13-21 cautions us not to put a stumbling block in a brother's way, or to do anything by which a brother is offended or made weak. Let's not allow the world to set our standards for us, and let's not cause one another to stumble just because we're having gym class.

PART III

Physical Fitness

CHAPTER 6

GENERAL FITNESS PRINCIPLES

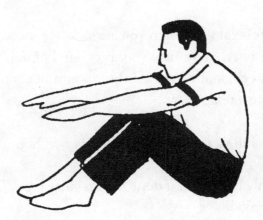

The following is a very general definition for physical fitness.

Definition. Physical fitness is the ability to carry out daily tasks comfortably, with ample energy to meet unexpected emergencies, keeping all bodily systems functioning properly with minimal degeneration.

Physical fitness (temple maintenance) is the core of our physical education program. The term "physical fitness" is a very *relative* term and is always a matter of degree. Most of us can choose how "fit" we want to be, and it all depends on how much time and effort we put into it. As Christians, we must consider the matter of "stewardship" in all we do, including physical fitness activities. The program suggested in this manual is presented with the hope that we will all achieve a reasonably good level of physical fitness and still be good stewards of our time and energies. This program may not make us fit enough to run a marathon or swim the English Channel, but we should be able to fulfill the definition given above and maintain God's temple.

General Benefits. Proper exercise that is suited to the individual can go a long way to slow down the aging process and help in stress management. It is a factor in the prevention of most of the major health problems of our day.

Fitness Program Do's and Don'ts.

1. When beginning a fitness program, start slowly and gradually increase the intensity and duration of your fitness activities. Excess *fatigue* and *soreness* are signs of *overdoing* it.

2. People with injuries should still exercise but avoid any specific exercise that aggravates the injury.

3. Sick people should not exercise at all. When you are sick, you need rest, not exercise. When the symptoms of your illness are gone, then resume your program but don't just pick up where you left off. Rather, start out slowly and gradually increase the amount of exercise over a period of days or weeks; otherwise, you may have a relapse.

4. It's best not to exercise on a full stomach. Waiting about two hours after eating is ideal.

5. Be consistent; exercise is only beneficial if done on a regular basis. Exercising only once a week can often do more harm than good.

6. Tailor-make an individualized fitness program for each individual according to his present level of ability.

7. Follow a balanced fitness program as described below.

A *Balanced Fitness Program*. It's not enough to just be a jogger, or a tennis player, or a swimmer. These activities can contribute to physical fitness, but they cannot be completely relied upon to maintain fitness. Just as there is no single food that meets all our nutritional needs, likewise, there is no single sport or fitness activity that provides for all our fitness needs. Even professional athletes, who spend most of their time playing their sport, still need a physical fitness program to maintain fitness. It is necessary to engage in a variety of activities to meet all our fitness needs. There are three specific types of exercise that provide balance: *aerobic* exercise, *strength* exercise, and *flexibility* exercise.

I recommend that all three types be included on a regular basis to provide a balanced fitness program. It is not necessary to include all three types for each gym class; they can be rotated and alternated to suit each family. We'll look at each of these separately.

CHAPTER 7

AEROBIC EXERCISE

Definition. Aerobic exercise is any type of exercise in which oxygen is not used faster than it can be supplied.

Description and Examples. Aerobic exercises are low intensity exercises that can be continued over an extended period of time. The intensity of the exercise is low enough to allow the body to continuously use oxygen to produce energy. This is different from "anaerobic" exercise, such as weight lifting or sprinting, in which the intensity of exertion is so high that the body must produce energy without oxygen. Anaerobic exercise can be continued for only a short period of time, while aerobic exercise can be continued for a long time.

Some examples of aerobic exercise are jogging, swimming, sledding, jumping rope, cross-country skiing, stair climbing, mountain climbing, ice and roller skating, trampoline bouncing, brisk walking, biking, calisthenics and many work activities. Any activity that keeps the heart rate continuously elevated is an aerobic activity.

How Long/How Often. As part of a balanced fitness program, some kind of aerobic exercise should be performed at least **three times each week for twelve to sixty minutes,** depending on the intensity of the activity and the fitness level of the individual. The more intense the exercise, the less time is necessary to gain the full benefits. Running is by far the most effective, efficient and convenient aerobic activity. Twelve minutes of running is sufficient to gain a good aerobic effect; it takes about twenty-five minutes of swimming, thirty-five minutes of biking, or fifty minutes of a vigorous game like basketball to give the same benefits.

If you do not practice a balanced fitness program, and aerobics is the only type of exercise that you do, then the aerobic program being suggested here would not be sufficient to maintain cardiovascular fitness. Instead, you would need to do 20 to 30 minutes of aerobic exercise at least three times each week. But if your aerobic exercise is coupled with the other types of exercise given in this manual, as little as 12 minutes will be sufficient. This will be further explained in the Strength Exercise section of the manual.

Whatever aerobic activity you do, you must feel like you're working fairly hard; a leisurely stroll won't provide the benefits of aerobic exercise. Some fitness specialists recommend keeping track of your heart rate during aerobic exercise, but most feel that this is not necessary for people whose health is reasonably good. However, if you have a heart problem or any other serious medical condition, you may want to keep track of your heart rate during exercise; with such medical conditions you should begin an exercise program only under your doctor's supervision.

The elderly or those with a low level of fitness should stick with a very low-intensity activity, such as brisk walking. As the fitness level increases, change to a combination of jogging and walking, gradually increasing the jogging time and decreasing the walking time. A good rule of thumb is to increase your jogging time by no more than 10 percent each week.

Very young children should be encouraged to do what they can, but don't expect them to hold to a strict exercise program. You'll have to use your own judgment as to what to require from each child, depending on his present abilities. A six-year-old may be able to jog only one to three minutes without stopping, while a ten-year-old may go for twelve to fifteen minutes, or much longer.

Benefits. Aerobic exercise primarily improves the cardiovascular system, causing the heart and blood vessels to get bigger, stronger and more resilient. It also helps lower blood cholesterol, increases the body's ability to burn fat, increases lung capacity, aids the excretory system, increases resistance to sickness, improves sleep, strengthens and tones the muscles involved, and helps in stress management. Aerobic exercise (even moderate) has also been demonstrated to significantly increase longevity (life span) and is the most effective type of exercise for burning fat and weight control. As far as health is concerned, aerobic exercise is considered the most important type of exercise, due to its many positive effects.

AEROBIC ACTIVITIES

Listed below are some activities that produce the aerobic effect if they are continued for twelve to sixty minutes. You can perform one activity for the full length of time or combine two or more activities for the full length of time. The latter is often preferable, as it becomes less boring and works a greater number of muscle groups.

Work Activities. Many work activities can be aerobic, such as:

> Mowing the lawn (but not with a riding mower).

> Cutting, splitting, and stacking fire wood
> (if done by hand and at a continuously brisk pace).

> Digging, raking, shoveling, hoeing weeds, baling hay, etc.
> Any activity that steadily holds the heart rate up for an
> extended period of time is aerobic.

Biking. To achieve a good aerobic effect on a bike, you need to ride fairly hard. Whenever possible, ride where there is little traffic. If your bike has gears, stay in a gear that allows you to "spin" the pedals at a fast pace, about 100 revolutions per minute.

If you're doing a lot of biking, it might be wise to wear a safety helmet. If riding in the early morning, evening or at night, use a light and wear something fluorescent.

Safety rules should always be practiced when riding on the road. Bikers are obligated by law to obey the same rules as those driving cars. That means stopping for stop signs and red lights, yielding wherever indicated by signs, obeying speed limits, etc. Here are a few important rules that should be learned and practiced by bikers.

1. Always ride on the right side of the road, in single file, with the flow of traffic. Never ride on sidewalks, unless permitted by signs.

2. Obey all traffic signs and signals.

3. Use arm signals for stopping or turning, always keeping the right hand on the handlebars.

Left Turn - Hold the left arm straight out, pointing left.

Right Turn - Hold the left arm pointing straight up with the elbow bent at ninety degrees.

Stop - Hold the left arm straight, pointing down, at forty-five degrees to the body.

4. Keep your breaks and tires in good condition at all times.

Brisk Walking or Running. You don't need expensive footwear (like "pumps") for walking or running, but some sort of well-cushioned, comfortable, flexible sneaker or running shoe is good. Foot injuries are somewhat common among walkers and runners and are usually caused by improper fitting or worn out footwear.

Whenever possible stay on grass or dirt rather than pavement. If you can, choose a course over different types of terrain with hills, curves, etc., rather than a flat track. When walking or running on the road, keep on the left side, facing oncoming traffic.

Calisthenics Exercises. If you perform a series of calisthenics exercises in a row for twelve minutes or more with no rest between exercises, it will produce a good aerobic effect. See the section on Strength Exercises for descriptions of exercises.

Jumping Rope. The rope should be long enough so you can stand up straight on the middle of it while holding both ends. Try jumping forward, backwards, on one foot, while walking or jogging. For advanced jumpers, try "peppers," swinging the rope as fast as possible, doing one jump for each swing. Harder still, try "doubles," doing one jump for every two swings.

Step - up. Use a sturdy box six to twelve inches high, or use the bottom step on the stairs. At a pace fast enough to keep the heart rate elevated, simply step up left, then right, then step down left, then right, and repeat.

Trampoline. Some families have a full-sized trampoline, but mini-trampolines are a more common sight in households today, and they can be used for a fun aerobic activity. Running in place, simple bouncing, and jumping rope while bouncing can all be aerobic exercise if performed continuously for twelve minutes or more. Many of the stunts given in the Gymnastics unit can be done repetitively while bouncing for an aerobic exercise.

Skill Drills. Performing drills for some game skills requires a lot of running and can be used as aerobic exercise. Try dribbling a soccer ball or basketball back and forth across the playing area for part or all of your aerobic exercise period. You can also practice passing a ball back and forth while running across the playing area.

Vigorous Games. Just playing certain games that require a lot of running, such as full-court basketball or soccer, can take the place of your aerobic exercise. But watch for some children who tend to run as little as possible during a game; they need to do their running, too.

Aerobic Circuit. Set up several aerobic activities and have family members rotate from one to the next every minute or two. In our house we like to have one jumping rope, one bouncing on the trampoline, one running up and down the stairs and another on the step-up. We go for one minute, then rotate.

AEROBICS RESEARCH PROJECTS

Listed below are some academic research projects that will help children to understand how aerobic exercise affects their bodies.

Body Systems Project. Do a study on the structure and function of the cardiovascular and/or respiratory systems, the various organs involved, and draw, color and label diagrams of them.

Heart Rate Project. Have children write down their pulse rate while at rest, then during their aerobic exercise, and after it. The pulse can be felt on the neck, just beside the trachea (wind-pipe), or on the thumb side of the wrist.
Take the pulse every minute after the exercise period is finished to see how long it takes to get back to normal.

For older students, determine their Training Heart Rate (THR). This is done by using the following formula:

$$220 - (\text{your age}) \times .7 = \text{THR}$$

Using this formula, a fifteen-year-old should be exercising hard enough to keep his pulse rate right around 143 beats/min. during his aerobic exercise (a little higher or lower is fine). This is his Training Heart Rate; it is the safest and most beneficial pulse rate for him, although teenagers don't need to be too concerned about their THR; just middle-agers and older, since risk of heart trouble increases with age.

Exercise as a Controlling Factor. Compose a report on library articles covering the role of exercise in stress management, heart disease control, blood pressure control or weight control.

Body Composition Project. Here's a great project for children and parents alike, to determine if you really have your fat under control. Weighing yourself is not a good method for this, since the scale only tells you how many pounds you weigh; it does not tell you how much fat you have on your body. With the help of an instrument called a "skin-fold caliper," you can take measurements on the body to determine its composition. The calipers will tell you what percent of your body weight is fat and what percent is lean body mass. This is a very accurate method of determining if you are over-fat.

Skin-fold calipers are available from Flaghouse equipment supplier for about $14.00. See the Equipment section of the manual for further information about purchasing equipment.

CHAPTER 8

STRENGTH EXERCISE

Definition. Any type of exercise in which the muscles work against some form of resistance is a strength exercise. A complete description of specific strength exercises can be found at the end of this chapter.

Description and Examples. Strength exercises are usually performed by lifting a weight against gravity. Weight training is the most effective type of strength exercise, but it requires a lot of expensive equipment that clutters up the house and can be dangerous.

Another type of strength exercise is called isometrics. Here, one presses against an immovable object with no motion at the joints. Although this requires no equipment and is very convenient, it is also the least effective type of strength exercise.

A good alternative for home schoolers is calisthenics: push-ups, pull-ups (chin-ups), sit-ups, rope climbing, etc. Calisthenics are almost as effective at increasing muscular strength as weight training. With calisthenics we can develop a balanced program that will work all the major muscle groups, using our own body weight for resistance. The only equipment needed are a few common household items and a chin-up bar. You can hang a bar in your cellar, garage, a doorway, or outside on a porch, in a tree or swing set.

Most of the work activities mentioned in the aerobics section will also contribute to muscular strength and tone. However, work activities should not be totally relied upon for fitness, since they are usually not balanced and may tend to over-work some muscle groups and under-work others.

A Balanced Strength Routine. We have about 600 muscles in the body, and they all need exercise. Fortunately, we don't have to perform 600 different exercises to work them all, since they work in groups, rather than individually. We can divide the skeletal muscles into seven major groups to pretty well cover them all. A balanced strength exercise routine will include at least one exercise to work each of the seven major muscle groups. (See the charts of Muscle Groups and Main Muscles at the end of this section.)

Benefits. Strength exercises are designed primarily to maintain and increase muscular strength and tone (firmness). In addition, they strengthen the bones and joints, help prevent injuries, and contribute (to some degree) to all of the benefits of aerobic exercise.

How Often. Strength exercises should be performed two or three times each week. It is best if we don't allow more than three days to pass without doing strength exercises, as the progress we have made begins to diminish after seventy-two hours.

From time to time it may be difficult to be consistent with our exercise program, especially if we go away on a trip or to a home-schooling seminar, etc. That's all right; we won't suffer permanent loss if we miss a week of exercise. If we've been consistent with our exercise program as a rule, then we can get right back to it after a week-long break and quickly regain whatever was. Occasional breaks are even good to take, since most of us begin to feel a bit "stale" after several months of an unbroken routine. But, as a rule, consistency is very important.

Repetitions and Sets. To perform an exercise one time, such as doing one push-up, is called one "repetition." When we repeat the exercise for several repetitions in a row, that is called a "set."

Beginners should be required to do only about ten repetitions for each muscle group. As progress is made, gradually add repetitions until you work up to thirty to fifty repetitions for each muscle group. This is sufficient to maintain a good level of physical fitness.

It is not necessary to do all the repetitions in one set, nor to do the same specific exercise for thirty to fifty repetitions. For example, you don't have to do thirty sit-ups in a row to work the abdominal muscles. Instead, you could do ten sit-ups, ten hanging knee raises, and ten L seats. It is actually better to do a variety of exercises for each muscle group whenever possible; this provides even better balance and works muscles from different angles. (It also gets less boring.)

Individualized Routines. Each individual should have his own strength exercise routine, designed according to his capabilities. At the end of this section you will find a reproducible Strength Exercise Chart. You will need one copy of the chart for each individual.

You will also find at the end of this section a list of descriptions of the strength exercises for all the major muscle groups. Read these descriptions as you choose exercises for each individual.

STRENGTH EXERCISE CHART FOR _____			
MUSCLE GROUP	BEGINNERS	INTERMEDIATE	ADVANCED
Chest and Arm extensors	Incline push-ups Modified push-ups Jump dips	Push-ups Modified dips	Raised push-ups Dips Handstand push-ups
Upper back and Arm flexors	Jump pull-ups Upright rowing light weight	Rowing motion	Pull-ups Upright rowing heavy weight
Abdominals	Beginner's sit-ups Hanging Knee raise Supported Knee raise	Modified sit-ups	Twist sit-ups Chair sit-ups Hanging Leg raise L-seat
Lower back	Arm and Leg raise Leg extension		
Hips and Thighs	Half squat	Squat thrust	Alternate Squat jump
Calf muscles	Toe raise	Full Toe raise	Single Toe raise
Shin muscles	Heel raise	Full Heel raise	Single Heel raise

The following are some guidelines for filling out each child's exercise chart, designing individualized routines and carrying each individual along as he progresses.

Beginner Level. Write the child's name at the top of his Strength Exercise Chart. Have him try one of the beginner exercises for each muscle group and write in the number of repetitions he is able to do correctly. Circle on the chart one exercise for each muscle group that is easy enough for him to do at least ten repetitions without too much strain. In total, you will have only seven different exercises, which is a good start for any beginner, regardless of age. The child can follow the chart each day, performing the seven different exercises that have been circled on his chart. Beginners need to be corrected often as they tend to forget some of the finer points of using correct technique while exercising.

As the weeks go by and this routine becomes easy, encourage the child to try to do a few more repetitions of each exercise. As progress is gradually made, and the child is able to perform fifteen or twenty repetitions of each exercise without too much difficulty, he's ready to go on to the intermediate level. It may take weeks, months or years to advance from one level to another, depending on the individual. Don't rush.

Intermediate Level. Continue the beginner routine as before, but add one new exercise to it for one muscle group. Choose the new exercise from either the beginner or intermediate category and perform five or ten repetitions to start, adding repetitions gradually. Every few weeks (perhaps once a month) add another new exercise until the child develops a second full routine. At this point the child will perform his beginner routine first, and then his intermediate routine. When the child is able to do about fifteen repetitions of each exercise in both routines without too much difficulty, he is ready to go on to the advanced level.

Don't forget to keep an eye on the child while he performs his exercises to make sure he's using correct technique.

Advanced Level. Choose two or more exercises for each muscle group from any category of exercises, and perform ten to twenty repetitions of each, one after another. You will no longer do one complete routine, and then start a second. At this level you will do two or more exercises for the same muscle group right in a row before going on to the next muscle group. For example, for the hips and thighs, do fifteen squat thrusts, fifteen alternate squat jumps and fifteen half squats, all right in a row with no rest or other exercises in between. This provides intensive work for the muscle group and is very effective for increasing muscular strength, tone and endurance. When one muscle group is finished, then go on to another. Arrange the exercises for each muscle group by placing the most difficult exercises first.

As each individual progresses and the routine becomes easier, substitute more advanced exercises, or add repetitions. A total of thirty to fifty repetitions for each muscle group is plenty of exercise for anyone. Some advanced people will have the ability to do more than fifty repetitions for a particular muscle group, but this is not necessary for maintaining a good level of physical fitness. Let's not get carried away with exercise so that it becomes a source of pride and causes us to become poor stewards of our time and energy.

Poster Board Charts. Rather than having your children follow the reproducible paper charts provided in the manual to do their exercises, you may want to write each child's list of exercises in big lettering on a poster board and mount it in your exercise room. A big poster is easy to follow from a distance, which will help the children to move quickly from one exercise to the next.

Age Differences. Strength exercises can be very beneficial for the elderly but should be done only after consulting a doctor.

Very young children should not be required to do strength exercises until, in your judgment, they are physically mature enough. Typically, they can start an easy beginner's routine around six or seven years of age. At this age children should not be pushed, as excessively hard training can cause permanent damage to their developing bones, joints and muscles. If it's fairly easy for them to do the exercises, then it's OK.

<u>Proper Technique</u>. Here are a few do's and don'ts for strength exercises. Perform each repetition:

1. <u>smoothly</u> - no jerking or swinging.
2. <u>rhythmically</u> - no long resting between repetitions.
3. <u>thoroughly</u> - moving the joints through their full range of motion without cheating. For example, with each pull-up, we should begin with straight arms, pull the chin over the bar, and return to straight arms. Cheating gives less benefit and can develop muscles improperly if continued for a long time. One exception is squats; doing full squats can aggravate injuries of the knee joint, so half-squats are recommended.

4. <u>with proper breathing</u>. Exhale during the hardest part of the motion, when pushing or pulling against gravity. Inhale during the easiest part of the motion, when lowering with gravity.

5. <u>remembering</u> that your goal is not to break the world's record for speed or the number of repetitions. Your goal is to work each muscle group thoroughly and properly.

One More Benefit. There is one last plus for the strength exercise routine. It can also provide a good degree of aerobic effect for the cardiovascular system if the exercises are performed with no extended rest between repetitions or sets.

This requires some self discipline but is very beneficial. First, it enables us to be good stewards of our time since it will take less time to do the strength exercises this way. Second, it enables us to spend less time on aerobic exercise. If we begin our aerobic exercise period immediately after completing our strength exercises, then we only need to do aerobics for twelve minutes or so. Without the aerobic effect from the strength exercises, we would have to do twenty to thirty minutes of aerobic exercise. So we can get double benefits from strength exercises if we do them without resting between repetitions or sets and then move right into our aerobic exercise period.

What About Becoming Muscle Bound? The program being suggested in this manual will not turn your sons into hulking muscle-men, as that requires years of intensive weight training. Neither will this program develop big, ugly muscles on girls, since girls don't have the necessary hormones, although it will increase muscular strength. We should recognize that there is nothing unfeminine about girls developing muscular strength. When speaking of the "virtuous woman," Proverbs 31, verse 17 says, "She girdeth her loins with strength, and strengtheneth her arms." Additional strength is an advantage for any girl or woman trying to keep up with household duties.

Strength Exercise Research Projects. Do a study on the structure and function of muscles and the muscular system. Study what actually happens within muscle tissue as it becomes stronger. Study the digestive system and how food is actually transformed into living tissue in your body. Study the nerves that stimulate the muscles, tracing them back to the brain. Include colored and labeled drawings and diagrams.

MAJOR MUSCLE GROUPS

Front View

Back View

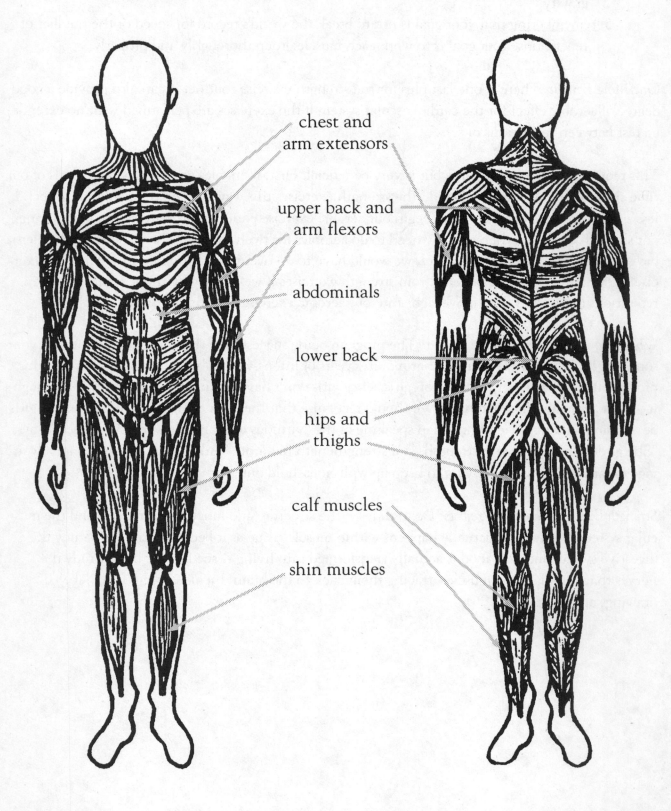

chest and
arm extensors

upper back and
arm flexors

abdominals

lower back

hips and
thighs

calf muscles

shin muscles

Muscles

Front View

Back View

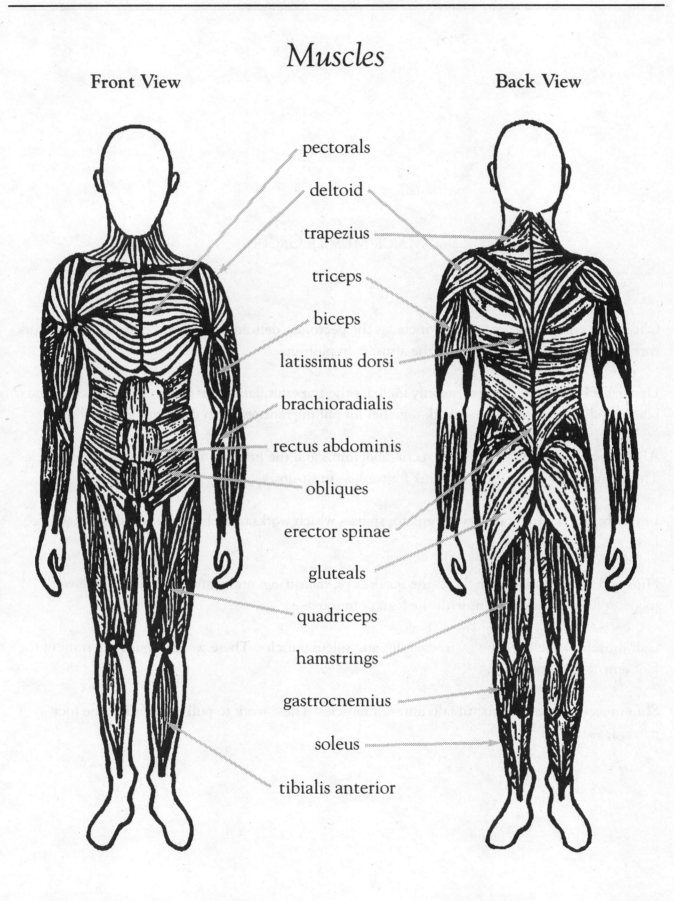

pectorals

deltoid

trapezius

triceps

biceps

latissimus dorsi

brachioradialis

rectus abdominis

obliques

erector spinae

gluteals

quadriceps

hamstrings

gastrocnemius

soleus

tibialis anterior

Major Muscle Groups

Chest and arm extensors - mainly includes the pectorals, deltoid, and triceps muscles. These work together for pushing motions with the arms, as in push-ups.

Upper back and arm flexors - mainly includes the trapezius, latissimus dorsi, deltoid, biceps, and brachioradialis muscles. These work together for pulling motions with the arms, as in pull-ups.

Abdominals - mainly includes the rectus abdominis and the internal and external oblique muscles. These work together to curl the trunk forward, as in sit-ups.

Lower back - mainly includes the erector spinae, which works to arch the back, as in arm and leg raises.

Hips and thighs - mainly includes the quadriceps, hamstrings and gluteal muscles. These work together for pushing motions with the legs, as in squats.

Calf muscles - includes the gastrocnemius and soleus muscles. These work to push the front of the foot down, as in toe raises.

Shin muscles - includes the tibialis anterior muscles. These work to pull the front of the foot upward, as in heel raises.

STRENGTH EXERCISE DESCRIPTIONS

CHEST AND ARM EXTENSORS

Beginners

Modified Push-ups. Lie face down and push up to a straight arm position. The back remains straight, and the knees remain on the floor. Then return, touching the chin to the floor and back up again.

Jump Dips. Place the hands on the sawhorses. Jump up and push up to a straight arm support, then lower down slowly.

Incline Push-ups. Place the hands on the edge of a sturdy table. Move the feet back until the body is inclined at about forty-five degrees. Push up to a straight arm position and return. The body remains straight.

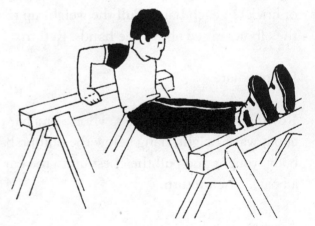

Intermediate

Push-ups. Lie face down, keeping the whole body straight. Push up to a straight arm position, then return, touching the chin to the floor. The back and knees remain straight.

Modified Dips. Place the hands behind you on a sawhorse. Rest the feet on another in front. Bend at the waist, bend the arms, and lower the body down. Push up to a straight arm position and repeat. (Chairs can be used instead of sawhorses.)

Advanced

Raised Push-ups. Place the feet on a chair and the hands on two chairs or sawhorses. Keep the body straight, and lower the chest between the hands, then push up to a straight arm position.

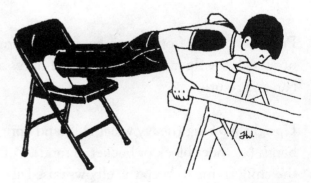

Dips. Support the body weight on the hands on the sawhorses. Bend the knees and keep them bent. Lower the body until the shoulders come close to the hands. Push up to a straight arm position.

Handstand Push-ups. Place the hands on the floor several inches from a wall. Kick up to a handstand, and let the feet rest against the wall. Lower the body slowly until the head touches the floor. Push back up to a handstand.

Upper Back and Arm Flexors

Where single asterisks (*) appear, it is good to alternate hand grips. Do half of the repetitions with the over-grip (palms facing front) and half with the under-grip (palms facing yourself).

Beginners

Jump pull-ups.* Use a pull-up bar that is a little above the head. Hold the bar and jump, pulling the chin over the bar. Hold the chin over the bar for two seconds, then lower down slowly. (Parents can give assistance by holding the feet, legs or hips and pushing up only as much as necessary.)

Upright Rowing (light weight). Stand upright and hold a weight (book or brick) in each hand. Pull the weight up to the chin, trying to keep the elbows raised above the hands. Return.

Intermediate

Rowing Motion.* Using a sawhorse or a bar placed about waist height, hang below the pull-up bar. Keep the body straight and pull the chest up to the bar (as if rowing a boat). Then return.

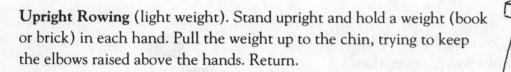

Advanced

Pull-ups.* Hang from a high bar with the arms straight; the feet should not touch the floor (bend the knees if necessary). Pull the chin over the bar, and return.

Upright Rowing (heavy weight). Stand upright, holding a weight in the hands (a cinder block or bucket of sand). Pull up until the hands reach the chin, trying to keep the elbows raised above the hands. Return.

ABDOMINALS

Where double asterisks (**) appear, these exercises should always be done while trying to keep the feet flat on the floor. At first you may need to have a partner hold the feet down or hook them under something, but, as soon as you can, do the exercise with no assistance. Keep the knees bent at approximately ninety degrees. Curl the chin to the chest with each repetition, and do not arch the back at any time during these exercises.

Beginners

Beginner's Sit-ups.** Lie on the back with the arms overhead. Swing the arms forward, reaching past the knees. Sit up, trying to touch the chest to the knees. Return slowly.

Hanging Knee Raise. Hang from a high bar. Keeping the arms straight pull the knees up as high as possible. Return slowly.

Supported Knee Raise. Support the body between the sawhorses. Keep the arms straight, and raise the knees as high as possible. Return slowly.

Intermediate

Modified Sit-ups.** Lie on the back and cross the arms on the chest. Sit up and extend the elbows over the knees, trying to touch the chest to the knees. Return slowly.

Advanced

Twist Sit-ups.** Lie on the back and place the fists next to the ears, or cross the arms behind the neck (do not interlock the fingers behind the neck). Twist while sitting up and pass the right elbow over the left knee. Return slowly and repeat while twisting to other side.

Chair Sit-ups** Lie on the back and place the lower legs on a chair seat. Sit up, trying to touch the chest to the knees. Return slowly.

Hanging Leg Raise. Hang from a high bar, keeping the arms and knees straight. Raise the ankles to the bar. Return slowly.

"L" Seat. Support the body weight on the hands on the sawhorses. Keep the arms and knees straight and raise the legs to ninety degrees at the hips. Return slowly.

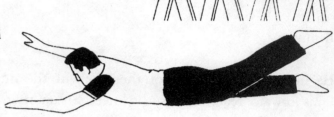

LOWER BACK

Beginners

Alternate Arm + Leg Raise. Lie face down with the arms stretched overhead. Keep the knees straight and raise the right leg and left arm. Return slowly, then raise the other arm and leg.

Leg Extension. Kneel on all fours and slowly extend one leg back and up, keeping the back straight. Lower the leg slowly, and repeat the same leg for a full set. Then switch to the other leg.

HIPS AND THIGHS

Beginners

Half Squat. Stand with the feet shoulder-width and place the hands on the hips. Squat half-way down and extend the arms straight in front, keeping the head up, back straight and feet flat on the floor. The knees should bend only to ninety degrees. Return to standing.

Intermediate

Squat Thrust. Stand straight, squat and place the hands on the floor. Jump the feet back to a push-up position. Return the feet to a squat position and then stand up straight.

Advanced

Alternate Squat Jump. Place the hands on the hips and the left foot in front. Bend the right knee to the floor, then jump up and switch the feet in the air. When you land, gently lower the left knee to the floor and repeat.

CALF MUSCLES

Beginners

Toe Raise. Stand straight with the feet flat. Raise up high on the tiptoes and return. (You may need to hold something to keep your balance.)

Intermediate

Full Toe Raise. Place the balls of the feet on the edge of a step. Lower the heels below the step level, then raise up high on the tiptoes, and return.

Advanced

Single Toe Raise. Place the ball of the left foot on a step and have no weight on the right foot. Lower the heel below the step level, then raise up high on the tiptoes. Return and repeat for a full set, then switch to the right foot.

SHIN MUSCLES

Beginners

Heel Raise. Stand straight with the feet flat. Lift the front of the foot up and raise up high on the heels, then return. (You may need to hold something to keep your balance.)

Intermediate

Full Heel Raise. Place the heels on the edge of a step.
Lower the front of the feet below the step level, then raise up high on the heels and repeat.

Advanced

Single Heel Raise. Place the left heel on the edge of a step, putting no weight on the right foot. Lower the front of the left foot below the step level, then raise up high on the left heel. Return and repeat for a full set, then switch to the right foot.

STRENGTH EXERCISE CHART
FOR _____

MUSCLE GROUP	BEGINNERS	INTERMEDIATE	ADVANCED
Chest and Arm extensors	Incline push-ups Modified push-ups Jump dips	Push-ups Modified dips	Raised push-ups Dips Handstand push-ups
Upper back and Arm flexors	Jump pull-ups Upright rowing light weight	Rowing motion	Pull-ups Upright rowing heavy weight
Abdominals	Beginner's sit-ups Hanging Knee raise Supported Knee raise	Modified sit-ups	Twist sit-ups Chair sit-ups Hanging Leg raise L seat
Lower back	Arm and Leg raise Leg extension		
Hips and Thighs	Half squat	Squat thrust	Alternate Squat jump
Calf muscles	Toe raise	Full Toe raise	Single Toe raise
Shin muscles	Heel raise	Full Heel raise	Single Heel raise

CHAPTER 9

FLEXIBILITY EXERCISE

Definition. Exercises which maintain and improve the range of motion of the joints are flexibility exercises.

Description and Examples. When performing a flexibility exercise (such as toe touches), we stretch a joint or group of joints as far as possible and hold there for ten to thirty seconds. Most flexibility exercises will stretch a number of joints at the same time, so it doesn't take too many exercises in a routine to cover all the major joints.

The beginner's routine at the end of this section contains all the exercises necessary for a balanced flexibility program. This routine can be used for any age group or level of fitness. Some advanced flexibility exercises are also included for those who may wish (or need) to do more intensive stretching.

How Long. Beginners should hold each stretch for ten seconds. After two or three months of consistent stretching, increase to twenty seconds. After another two or three months, increase to thirty seconds; that's as long as anyone needs to hold each stretch.

How Often. To maintain good flexibility it is only necessary to perform the routine two or three times each week. However, it is advisable to use flexibility exercises as part of a warm-up and cool-down for any demanding physical activity, whether the activity is work, exercise or recreation. (See the *Lesson Procedure* section in chapter 4 of the manual.) If you use the routine this way, to start and finish each physical education class, you need not do any additional stretching.

Proper Technique. Here are a few do's and don'ts for flexibility exercises.

1. Walk briskly and/or jog for one or two minutes before stretching. This helps prevent injury from stretching muscles before they're warmed up.

2. Relax, breathing slowly and deeply.

3. Stretch slowly, as far as <u>you</u> can go, and hold. Don't compare yourself to others; it only matters that you stretch to your own limit.

4. Don't bounce; this can decrease your flexibility rather than increase it.

5. Don't have someone else stretch you by pushing you down; always stretch yourself.

6. Don't stretch so far that it causes excruciating pain. Stretch only far enough to feel slight discomfort.

Benefits. Flexibility exercises are primarily designed to keep the joints free-moving. In so doing, they also help to prevent injuries and soreness and speed recovery from the same. They also help to improve blood circulation and relieve tension and stress.

Americans miss more work days due to back trouble than any other cause. One of the greatest benefits of flexibility exercises is their ability to prevent and treat back trouble.

Flexibility Research Projects. Do a study on the skeletal system. Study the structure and function of bones. Examine the different types of joints and how they are constructed. Draw, color and label diagrams of the bones and joints, including the ligaments and tendons that hold them together.

FLEXIBILITY EXERCISES

Beginners Routine

Ankle, Thigh and Shoulder Stretch. Kneel down and sit on the ankles, keeping the feet pointing straight back. Place the hands close together on the floor, palms down, as far behind as possible. Hang the head back and hold.

Toe Stretch. Same as above, but instead of pointing the toes back, bend the toes so that you are resting on the balls of the feet.

Toe Touch. Sit on the floor with the knees straight and feet together. Lower the head and chest as far down toward the knees as possible. Reach the hands as far down the legs as possible, trying to touch the toes. If you can't reach your toes, just hold on to your ankles, pull gently and hold.

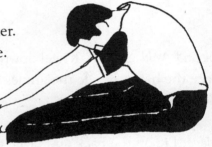

Repeat the same as above, but this time push the heels out and pull the toes back toward you and hold.

Arch-up Stretch. Lie face down, raise the head up, and arch back, looking at the ceiling. Place the hands on the floor under the shoulders and push up, still arching back as far as possible and keeping the hips on the floor. Hold.

Fold-up Stretch. Kneel down and sit on the ankles with the feet pointing straight back. Bend forward and lay the chest on the thighs. Reach the arms straight overhead with the palms on the floor and lower the head toward the floor. Hold.

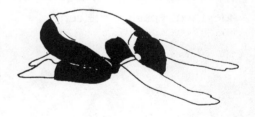

Straddle Stretch. Sit on the floor with the feet as far apart as possible. Keep the knees straight and bend the chest and head toward one knee. Reach both hands as far as possible down one leg, pull gently and hold. Repeat on the other leg. Repeat a third time in the center, holding both ankles, pulling the chest and head toward the floor.

Cross-Over Stretch. Lie on the back with the arms straight out to the sides. Raise the right leg up and cross it over to the left side, keeping the shoulders on the floor and knees straight. Try to place the right foot as close to the left hand as possible and hold. Repeat to the other side.

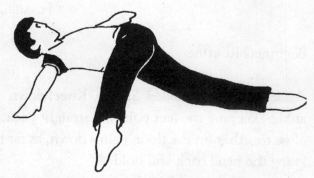

Shoulder Stretch. Hang by the hands from a pull-up bar, relax the shoulders and hold.

ADVANCED STRETCHES

Toe and Ankle Stretch. Kneel down and sit on the ankles, keeping the feet pointing straight back. Place the hands beside the ankles and push down, raising the knees up to bend the toes backwards and hold.

Bridge. Lie on the back and place the palms down beside the head, with the fingers pointing toward the shoulders. Bend the knees and keep the feet on the floor. Arch up and push the hips toward the ceiling. Push the arms and legs as straight as possible, forming a bridge shape with the body. Hold.

Splits. Stand with the feet as far apart as possible, and place the hands on the floor. Keeping the knees straight, roll one leg over and push the foot as far back as possible. Hold. Repeat to other side, then repeat to the center.

PART IV

ACTIVITIES

CHAPTER 10

SKILL DEVELOPMENT

Skill development and practice are necessary for everyone. Even professional athletes practice fundamental skills regularly, making fine adjustments in technique. For beginners, it's all the more important. Without basic skills, participation in any work or recreational activity becomes very frustrating. It is necessary to present skills in a logical progression and allow time for experimentation and practice. Once the basic skills are understood and mastered, the child is ready to use the skills to participate in an activity.

Benefits. Practicing skills accomplishes several other purposes beside gaining the skills necessary to perform work or play games. Skill practice improves hand-eye and foot-eye coordination and contributes to physical fitness. It may also enable a child to learn that all-important lesson in life: that he can learn to do most things he puts his mind to.

Breaking Skills Down. We usually take for granted the skills we already have, not realizing what it took to learn them. Just throwing a ball is a highly complex skill that involves many body parts doing different things at different times. Children should not be expected to perform such skills naturally; they need instruction and practice.

If a child can't perform a skill, simply break it down into its parts and have him perform one part at a time. The skill must be broken down to a level at which the child is able to *successfully* do what you ask. If the child can't catch a ball that is thrown to him, have him gently toss it up himself a few inches high and catch it. Gradually encourage him to toss it higher and higher. Then you toss it and have him catch it. Then back up a bit, and so on. If a child can't dribble a basketball with one hand, have him do it with two. Whatever you ask him to do, it must be easy enough for him to accomplish, yet difficult enough to challenge him. A good teacher always seeks this balance.

Maturity Limitations. Sometimes, no matter how much you work at a skill, a child may not be able to learn it simply because of his overall immaturity. Be careful about requiring skills that are beyond a child's reach. If you've broken a skill down as far as you can, and the child still can't do it, then he may not be mature enough for that skill yet. After he tries it a few times and fails, move on to something else that he *can* do. Later you can come back to the other skill and try it again.

You'll have to use your own discernment whether the child is truly unable to perform a skill, or whether he is just unsure of himself or doesn't feel like trying. We don't want to reward lack of effort, but neither do we want to discourage and frustrate a child with skills beyond his reach.

Skills in Lessons. Each unit that is presented in the Activities section of the manual has a list of "Related Skills." These specific skills are necessary for participation in that activity. For each lesson, it's good to first review one or two of the skills that the child has already mastered. Give some time to practice, watching for minor errors in technique. Next, present one new skill that the child may not know. Give time to experiment with the skill and practice it. Then, if there is a fair degree of mastery of the new skill, do the activity for the day using the new skill. If the child just can't learn the new skill yet, it's better not to have him participate in an activity that requires it.

Right and Left Handers. Allow a child to use the hand that comes naturally to him for all skills.

All skills presented in this manual will be described for right-handed players, with the understanding that left-handed players will perform the skill the same way, but to the other side.

Beginners Skills. For the beginners in the family, you should spend quite a bit of time in the following units:

> Basic Ball Skills
> Locomotor Skills
> Hand-Eye Coordination

These units contain the foundational skills for most other activities. There are some simple games that involve basic skills, but many times just practicing a new skill is activity enough for a beginner. It's not necessary to play a game right away using a new skill unless the child catches on to it fairly well.

Keep in mind that age doesn't matter here; a beginner is anyone who hasn't mastered the basics. There are plenty of high schoolers who dislike basketball because they never learned to dribble or shoot. Regardless of age, never leave basic skills behind.

CHAPTER 11

WORK ACTIVITIES

Physical Education doesn't have to be (indeed, should not be) all fun and games and exercises. It is perfectly acceptable and in line with our goals to include vigorous work activities as part of the physical education program. Many young people today don't know what it is to work; therefore, it is wise to include work activities as part of the program.

Of course, work activities that are not vigorous, such as washing dishes, would not be counted as physical education.

Substituting. On any given day, instead of doing strength exercises, you might substitute a chore that requires heavy lifting, such as splitting fire wood. Instead of doing an aerobic exercise, you might substitute a less intense chore that is continued for an extended period of time, such as mowing the lawn (of course, not with a riding mower.)

There are no work activities that can be substituted for flexibility exercises, so no matter how much hard physical labor you do, you'll still need to do stretching. But

most work activities do contribute to muscular strength and tone, and many chores can produce an aerobic effect too, if they are continued for an extended period of time. Gardening, mowing lawn, raking, shoveling snow, hoeing weeds, digging, baling hay, and cutting, splitting and stacking firewood are a few examples of good, vigorous, work activities that can be included in the physical education program.

One Caution. Work activities should not be totally relied upon for fitness, since they are usually not balanced and may tend to overwork some muscle groups and underwork others. After several hours of gardening, we often develop a sore back because that particular activity overworks the back muscles. But most other muscles usually aren't sore from gardening because those muscles get neglected; so we still need a fitness program to balance things.

In addition, we all have a natural tendency to try to find easier ways to do things and use labor-saving devices. There's nothing wrong with this, as it helps to save time and bodily energy and often saves money too. But the easier we make the job, the less fitness benefits we gain from it. So if you can afford the time, try doing a few chores the old way, such as cutting firewood with a bow saw.

Work Activities as Lessons. When using vigorous work activities as part of the physical education program, it's good to follow the usual Lesson Procedures given in the Planning section of the manual. For vigorous activities, include a warm-up period, review and instruction in skills, the chore itself, then a cool-down.

City Dwellers. Those who live in the city may not have the yard space for many work activities. If so, you might consider looking for some odd jobs for your children. See if a neighbor would be willing to pay them for mowing the lawn or shoveling snow from their driveway. Another alternative is to offer free help as a ministry to an elderly person, or a family that just had a baby, or a family that is moving to a new house. Learning to do and enjoy physical labor is an important part of a complete education, especially for city dwellers.

CHAPTER 12

ACTIVITY UNITS

Rather than doing different, unrelated recreational activities from day to day, it's better to work on one specific *activity unit*, such as basketball, for a period of about *two or three weeks*. During the unit you would cover various related skills as well as activities and games using those skills. That way students would learn and apply their skills much more efficiently. Present and practice one or two new skills each session, practice some old ones and select a game or activity that uses those skills.

Unit Length. Some activity units could be as brief as one class; others, you might want to run for three or four weeks; the choice is yours, depending on how far you want to go with each unit.

Unit Depth. The last section of the manual contains a number of activity units, listed alphabetically. These units cover the basic skills related to each activity and offer recreational games and activities using those skills. If you wish to pursue any activity units in greater depth, your local library should have books about them.

Choosing Units. You will have to decide which activity units, skills and work and recreational activities are appropriate for your family, according to each child's abilities and your own goals, equipment and facilities.

CHAPTER 13

GAME ORGANIZATION

Here are a few helpful hints about organizing games:

Setting Boundaries. Whenever possible, try playing games without specified boundaries. Games are much more enjoyable if we don't have to stop the play every time the ball goes over a boundary line, especially when we don't have a big athletic field. Just give a general encouragement to keep the ball in your own yard, and if it strays , whoever is closest to it can just bring it back into play without interrupting the game.

This won't always work, and sometimes you might find your players running unreasonable distances from the game location, into the neighbor's garden, etc. When this happens, you may have to set distinct boundary lines. For lines you can use ropes on the ground, garden hoses, or just mark the corners of the field with a rag, tree, etc.

For more permanent boundary marking, you can make lines with lime or spray a narrow strip of weed killer.

Making Teams. Never line your children up, appoint two captains and have them pick teams. The least-skilled players always get picked last and always feel rejected and unwanted. It's much better for the parent to just divide the group evenly and play.

Parental Participation. Parents are encouraged to participate in games to keep things running smoothly. If the teams are uneven, parents should play on the team that needs the most help (assuming you are more skilled than your children). You should help only enough to keep things even.

As mentioned in chapter 3, some games are difficult to change from competitive to cooperative, such as soccer. If you have only young children, have them play against you and play only hard enough to keep it challenging for them.

Another reason for parental participation is to provide the opportunity for encouragement. Give compliments liberally, especially if you have a child who is weak academically; gym class may be the one activity where he can shine. This may help him to discover that he can succeed elsewhere if he applies himself.

It's also a good idea to take each child aside privately and encourage him to compliment his brothers and sisters when they make a good play as well as when they try hard and fail. This helps reduce sibling rivalry and fosters cooperation and edification.

Playing Positions. Give each child equal opportunity to play different positions in all games. Be careful not to show favoritism to those who are more skilled, letting them always play the central positions.

With beginners, this may not always be possible. To ask a very young child to pitch in baseball would really hinder the game. In cases like this, it's better to let another player pitch, or perhaps the parent could be the pitcher for both teams. If a child is just not skilled enough to play a particular position, be sure to encourage him that the position he does play is important.

Indoor/Outdoor Games. Most games can be played either indoors or outdoors if modified enough. Nerf balls and balloons are usually not too destructive in the house as long as you have some open space and move fragile objects out of the way; just be careful about chandeliers. It's good to get out of the house as often as possible, so make every effort to have gym outside.

Limited Numbers of Players. Most of us aren't quite prolific enough to field twenty-two soccer players from our own family for an official game of soccer, so the games being presented in the activity units have been modified for families with a limited number of players. But sometimes it is nice to have bigger games, so you might consider getting together occasionally with another family for gym class.

CHAPTER 14

BADMINTON UNIT

Materials for Skill Practice--one badminton racquet for each player and one or more birdies (shuttlecocks).

RELATED SKILLS

Forehand Stroke. Stand sideways with the left foot in front, and draw the right arm back. As the birdie approaches on the right side, lean to the front, swat it by swinging the right arm a short way and snapping the wrist with the palm facing front. There is motion at the wrist and shoulder but little or no motion at the elbow.

Backhand Stroke. Stand sideways with the right foot in front and cross the right arm in front of the body. As the birdie approaches on the left side, lean to the front, swat it by swinging the right arm a short way and snapping the wrist with the palm facing the rear. There is motion at the wrist, elbow and shoulder.

Overhead Stroke. Whenever the birdie approaches above the head, it can be hit with either a forehand or backhand stroke, as described above.

Underhand Stroke. Whenever the birdie approaches below the waist, it can be hit with either a forehand or backhand stroke, with one difference: there is much less wrist action for any underhand stroke. The elbow and wrist are kept fairly straight, and there should be a good follow-through after the birdie is hit. (See the Basic Skills Unit, Chapter 16, for an explanation of "follow through.")

Serve. The player serving drops the birdie from his left hand and hits it over the net with either a forehand or underhand stroke.

GAMES AND ACTIVITIES

BADMINTON

Location. Outdoors

Players. 2 - 4

Materials. One badminton racquet for each player and one or more birdies. You can play with or without a net. Beginners may do better without a net and without boundaries.

Object. To hit the birdie back and forth as many times as possible.

To Play. Set the net about shoulder height with one or two players on each side. One player serves, and all players try to keep it going back and forth. When someone misses it, whoever picks up the birdie serves again.

CHAPTER 15

BASEBALL UNIT

RELATED SKILLS

See the Basic Ball Skills unit (chapter 16) for:
    throwing skills
    catching skills

Batting Technique. The batter stands to the side of home plate with his left shoulder toward the pitcher. The feet are about shoulder width apart and placed a foot or so away from home plate. The knees are slightly bent, and the face is turned to the pitcher. The hands are together with the right hand on top, and the bat is held above and behind the right shoulder.

The batter keeps his eyes on the ball and swings the bat on a level plane, being sure to follow through.

After hitting the ball, the bat is dropped straight down (not thrown), and the batter runs to first base.

Batting Skill. Hang a tether ball from a tree limb or swing set. Practice swinging and hitting the ball, using proper technique.

Glove Catch. (For a fly ball) Allow the ball to enter the open mitt, keeping the other hand just behind the mitt. Once the ball enters the mitt, use the other hand to quickly close the mitt to prevent the ball from popping out.

Grounder Catch. When the ball is rolling toward you, drop to one knee and place the fingertips of the open glove on the ground. Keep the other hand just above the glove with the palm facing the ground. When the ball enters the mitt, use the other hand to trap it inside.

Games and Activities

Scrub Baseball

Location. In or outdoors

Players. 2 - 10

Indoor Materials. A foam bat or short-handled paddle (such as a ping pong paddle or the family rod of correction), a nerf ball and two bases. (For bases use chalk marks on the floor, masking tape, cloths, etc.)

Outdoor Materials. A bat and ball of any kind and two bases. Use a regular softball, whiffle (plastic) ball, sock ball (roll up an old sock), nerf ball, big beach ball or any other kind of ball. For a bat use a regular bat, whiffle (plastic) bat, broom stick or paddle. For bases use marks in the dirt, cloths, square boards, tag a tree, etc.

Object. To hit a home run

To Play. Players rotate turns at bat while everyone else plays the field.

The pitcher pitches the ball with an underhand throw, making it easy to hit. The batter hits the ball and runs to first base, then back to home plate.

Fielders try to catch the ball and tag the batter before he makes it back to home plate. Fielders may pass the ball to one another or run while holding the ball to tag the runner. The ball may not be thrown at the runner; it must be held in the hands when tagging him.

Whether the batter makes it or not, he then becomes the pitcher; everyone else rotates positions, and a new player becomes the batter.

Notes and Variations
    —Don't count strikes; instead, give everyone all the strikes they need to get a fair hit.
    —Require advanced players to go farther to first base than everyone else.
    —Require fielders and batters to travel by different locomotor skills, such as hopping on one foot. (See the Locomotor Skills Unit, Chapter 25.)
    —Allow players to run closer to one another if necessary to make a good pass. If anyone misses a pass, he must run quickly to get the ball; no walking.
    —Use four bases and have the batter run all four bases after hitting the ball. The fielders must pass the ball to first, second, third and home before the runner makes it home.

PUNCHBALL

Played just like scrub baseball but using a big soft ball, such as a nerf ball or inflatable ball. The ball is pitched on one bounce, and the batter punches it and runs.

KICKBALL

Played just like scrub baseball, but the pitcher rolls the ball to the kicker who kicks it and runs.

Note. Little ones may not be able to kick a rolling ball, so place it on home plate for them to kick and shorten the distance to first base for them.

PICKLEBALL

Location. In or outdoors

Players. 3

Materials. One ball or bean bag (any size) and two bases (gloves are optional)

Object. To run from base to base as many times as possible without getting tagged

To Play. Place two bases throwing distance apart and station one baseman at each base. The basemen begin passing the ball back and forth. The runner begins in a "pickle" by standing between the two bases. He then tries to run to one base without getting tagged. If he makes it, he's safe as long as he stays on the base. He then continues to run from base to base as many times as possible without getting tagged.

The ball may not be thrown at the runner. A baseman may either hold the ball and chase the runner to tag him or pass the ball to the other baseman so he can tag the runner. When the basemen finally catch the runner, then everyone switches positions.

Note. If a player has a hard time making it to the bases, then require the basemen to travel by a more difficult locomotor skill. Runners should be able to make it several times before getting tagged. If the basemen have a really hard time catching the runner, then require the runner to travel by a more difficult locomotor skill.

CHAPTER 16

BASIC BALL SKILLS UNIT

Teaching Procedure. Beginners should be introduced to a variety of ball skills, one at a time, as follows:

1. Explain and demonstrate the proper technique involved in each skill.

2. Without a ball, go through the motions of the skill several times yourself.

3. Have the children go through the motions several times without a ball until they have the idea.

4. Give them the ball and have them practice the skill ten or twenty times.

5. If they're able to perform the skill, try a simple game in which they can use the new skills they've learned. If they are unable to perform the skill, teach them another simpler skill.

Follow-through. Whether throwing, kicking or hitting a ball (or any other object) follow-through is an important part of proper technique. After the ball is on its way, the body part that projects the ball must continue to move toward the target as far as possible. This helps to create a smooth motion and improves power and accuracy. For example, when kicking a soccer ball, the foot does not stop moving as soon as it hits the ball. Rather, the foot continues to move toward the target until the leg is fully extended. Be watchful for follow-through in all skills, always reminding players about it.

BEGINNER CATCHING SKILLS

Big nerf balls or inflatable gym balls are easiest for beginners. Present skills in the order they are given below.

Toss and Catch. Hold the ball with both hands. Toss the ball straight up a short way and catch it with both hands.

When this becomes easy, gradually encourage the child to toss the ball higher. Make it more challenging by having him clap while the ball is in the air. As this becomes easy, increase the number of claps.

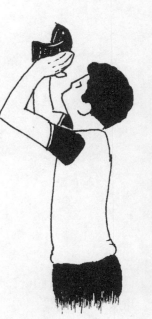

Note. Once the toss and catch can be done successfully, go on to other big ball skills. When first learning to catch a ball thrown by someone else, the person throwing the ball should stand very close and toss the ball straight up very gently. Gradually back up, working toward a more horizontal throw.

Two-Handed Catch (big ball). Let the ball hit both hands and pull the ball to the chest.

Two-Handed Catch (small ball). Try to trap the ball between the hands. The ball does not hit the chest.

Scoop Catch. To make a scoop, cut the bottom off a plastic, one-gallon milk jug. Have children practice catching a small ball with the scoop. Scoops can be used in many ball games.

THROWING SKILLS

The target for all throwing skills is the chest of the person to whom you are throwing.

All skills will be described for right-handed players, with the understanding that left-handed players will perform the skill the same way, but to the other side.

Remember to encourage a good follow-through after the ball leaves the hand for each throw.

Two-Handed Underhand Throw. Hold a big ball with both hands. Place the feet about shoulder width apart and bend the knees a little. Lower the ball between the knees, then toss the ball forward.

Chest Pass. Step either foot in front of the other and lean forward. Hold a big ball in both hands with the fingers spread. Place the backs of the hands against the chest and quickly push both arms straight in front to throw the ball.

One-Handed Underhand Throw. Step the left foot in front and lean forward. Keeping the arms almost straight, swing the right hand down and back while swinging the left hand in front. (Now you're ready to throw.) Swing the arms in opposite directions, keeping the right arm in a vertical plane to throw the ball.

Overhand Throw. Step the left foot in front and lean forward. Reach the left arm in front (pointing it toward the target) while moving the right hand behind the ear. (Now you're ready to throw.) Move the arms in opposite directions so the left elbow pushes back and the right arm straightens out, staying in a vertical plane to throw the ball. (Avoid sidearm throws.)

Bounce Pass. Use any of the above passes and make the ball hit the floor about half way between the partners.

Wall Pass. Stand several feet from a wall. Using any of the above passes, bounce the ball off the wall and catch it repeatedly.

DRIBBLING SKILLS

Use a big inflatable ball that bounces well. Encourage children to use their fingers to dribble instead of palms. This takes a while to learn since beginners tend to slap the ball with their palms, so give them some time to catch on. Dribbling skills should first be learned while trying to stay in one place, keeping the ball under control. Present dribbling skills in the order given below.

Two-Handed Bounce and Catch. Hold the ball in both hands. Bounce it and catch it with both hands.

Two-Handed Dribble. Repeatedly bounce the ball by hitting it with both hands.

One-Handed Dribble. Repeatedly bounce the ball with one hand, then try the other.

Alternate Dribble. Dribble once with the right hand; then left, then right, etc.

Low Dribble. See how low the child can keep dribbling.

High Dribble. See how high the child can keep dribbling.

Moving Dribble. Perform all the above dribbling skills while walking, running, shuffling sideways around obstacles, moving backwards and spinning in circles.

Double Dribble. For advanced players, try dribbling two balls, one with each hand. Then try dribbling both balls with one hand.

KICKING SKILLS

Use a big inflatable ball or firm nerf ball. Have children practice various kicks with each other or the parent, passing the ball back and forth. For individual practice, kick the ball against a wall.

To learn all kicking skills, place the ball on the ground so it doesn't move until it is kicked.

Basic Kicking technique. For any kick (unless otherwise specified), the non-kicking foot is always planted to the left side and just behind the ball. The knee is slightly bent, toes pointing toward the target.

The ankle of the kicking foot is always held firm in its kicking position. The kicking leg always follows through to a complete extension after the ball is kicked.

Toe Kick. Hold the kicking foot level and pointing straight ahead. Kick the center of the ball with the toe.

Instep Kick. Point the toe of the kicking foot downward and kick the ball with the instep or top of the foot. The shoe laces should make contact with the ball.

Inside Foot Kick. Hold the kicking foot level, with the knee slightly bent and toe pointed out. Kick with the inside of the foot.

Outside Foot Kick. Place the non-kicking foot behind and to the left side of the ball, with the toe pointing out. Kick with the outside of the other foot.

Heel Kick. Stand with your back to the ball and feet just in front of it. Kick the ball backward with your heel.

Punt. Hold the ball in both hands and extend the arms almost straight. Drop (do not toss) the ball while stepping forward onto the left foot and kick with the top of the right foot.

MISCELLANEOUS SKILLS

For a little fun and challenge, try tossing the ball up and bouncing it off various body parts, such as the head, shoulder, elbow, wrist, chest, back, hip, knee, etc. See what the children can come up with for different ways to bounce and propel the ball.

GAMES AND ACTIVITIES

BACKUP

Location. In or outdoors

Players. 2 to 8

Materials. One ball, any size

Object. To pass and catch the ball as many times as possible without dropping it

To Play. Arrange players in a small circle. Toss the ball around the circle from player to player, skipping no one. As soon as the ball goes all the way around the circle, everyone backs up one step. Continue until you get so far apart that it's difficult to catch.

Note. For beginners, allow them to catch the ball on one bounce. Try this game using various throwing skills.

BLANKET BALL

Location. In or outdoors

Players. 2 or more

Materials. A blanket, sheet, or parachute, and one or more balls. Balls may be any size from ping pong balls to beach balls.

Object. To make the ball(s) pop up or roll; to pass with accuracy

To Play. Spread out a big blanket on the ground and space children evenly around it. Everyone grabs the edge of the blanket and lifts together, pulling it tight. Place one or more balls on the blanket and pop them up, roll them and shake them around. Try to pass to one another or try to shoot into a basket.

Note. When the children get tired of this, have everyone lift the blanket overhead, step under and pull it down behind them like a tent.

CALL BALL

Location. Outdoors

Players. 3 to 10

Materials. One ball

Object. To catch the ball when your name is called

To Play. Arrange all players in a circle. Select one player to be the "caller." He stands in the middle, calls someone's name, tosses the ball straight up and moves out of the center. The player he calls must run in and try to catch the ball. He then gets to be the "caller."

Note. For beginners, allow them to catch the ball on one bounce. For advanced players, make the circle bigger and/or require them to use a different locomotor skill to move in to make the catch, or have them catch with one hand.

CIRCLE PASS

Location. In or outdoors

Players. 3 to 10

Materials. Two or more balls

Object. To see how many balls you can keep moving around the circle

To Play. Arrange all players in a circle. Begin passing one ball from player to player in one direction. Once one ball is moving well, begin a second ball in the same direction, then a third, etc. If someone misses, just pick it up right away and continue.

Variations.

    For extra challenge, try two balls going in opposite directions.
    Try different types of passes.

OTHER GAMES

See the Baseball unit for all games listed there.

See the Relay Race unit for:
    dribbling relays
    passing relays

See the Soccer unit for:
    speedball

See the Chase Games unit for:
    ball tag

CHAPTER 17

BASKETBALL UNIT

Indoor Materials. Use a big nerf ball or inflatable gym ball and a laundry or waste basket. Place the basket on the floor or in a chair.

Outdoor Materials. Use a regular basketball for older players and an inflatable gym ball that bounces well for younger players.

Use a regular basketball hoop or other large basket attached to a wall, pole, tree, etc. Set the basket a little higher than the child can reach without jumping.

RELATED SKILLS

See the Basic Ball Skills unit for:
>   catching skills
>   dribbling skills
>   throwing skills

Advanced Passing

For advanced players, try passing two balls between two players. One does a chest pass; the other does a bounce pass. If they can do this well, try three balls.

With three players, form a triangle and give each player a ball; all pass at the same time, either clockwise or counterclockwise.

With four players, form a square and have the players opposite each other passing back and forth.

Shooting Skills

One Hand Set Shot. Place the left hand under and in the front of the ball and the right hand behind it. Raise the ball above the head so that the back of the right hand is against the top of the fore-head, still keeping the eyes on the basket. Bend the knees, then rise up straight and shoot with the right hand. Be sure to follow through.

One Hand Jump Shot. Same as above, but jump as you shoot.

Two Hand Set Shot. Hold the ball with both hands. Raise it above the head, bend the knees a little and shoot.

Two Hand Jump Shot. Same as above, but jump as you shoot.

Granny Shot. Use a two-handed underhand toss to shoot.

Lay-up Shot. Run and dribble almost up to the basket. Leap and reach as high as possible. The arms merely lift the ball up to the rim, rather than shooting it up. Let the ball roll off the fingertips, bounce softly off the backboard and drop into the basket.

Hook Shot. Stand sideways with the left shoulder toward the basket. Holding the ball in the right hand, circle the right arm up with the elbow nearly straight, making a hooking motion. Pass the ball over the head toward the basket to shoot.

GAMES AND ACTIVITIES

FOLLOW THE LEADER

Location. In or outdoors

Players. 2 to 8

Materials. One or more balls and a basket

Object. To shoot a basket the same way the leader does

To Play. Ask the players to think of different ways to shoot. One player (the leader) shoots, and everyone else must shoot as he did, from the same spot. When everyone has had a turn, let someone else be the leader.

Note. Allow beginners to shoot from a closer position.

OBSTACLE BALL

Location. In or outdoors

Players. 1 to 8

Materials. One or more balls one basket and several obstacles.

Object. To dribble around obstacles and shoot a basket

To Play. Set up a number of obstacles, such as chairs, buckets, trash cans, etc. and designate a specific location from which to shoot. The parent shows the route the players must take to dribble up to the shooting location.

Variations. Use various dribbling and shooting skills as well as locomotor skills.

AROUND THE WORLD

Location. In or outdoors

Players. 1 to 8

Materials. One or more balls and a basket

Object. To score as many baskets as possible from several locations

To Play. Mark off several different locations on the floor or ground, going in a semi-circle around the basket. Players take turns shooting from each location, working their way around the circle. Each time they score, they move to the next location and shoot. If they miss, they continue shooting from that spot until they score.

Note. Make the distance from the basket a bit challenging but easy enough so they can score most of the time. Allow beginners to shoot from closer locations.

Variations. Try this game using each of the different shooting skills.

PASS AND SHOOT

Location. Outdoors

Players. 2 to 3

Materials. A ball and basket

Object. To move across the court by passing only and making the shot

To Play. Two or three players start at the far end of the court. They pass the ball back and forth while moving toward the basket without dribbling or running while carrying the ball. When they get close enough, one player shoots. If the shot misses, they quickly get the rebound and shoot again. If they score, they start over. See how many times in a row you can keep the ball under control and make the shot on the first try.

OTHER ACTIVITIES

See the Relay Races unit for:
    dribbling relays
    passing relays

See the Chase Games unit for:
    dribble tag

CHAPTER 18

CHASE GAMES UNIT

RELATED SKILLS

See the Locomotor Skills unit for different ways to move while playing some of these games, especially for indoor play.

GAMES AND ACTIVITIES

CROWS AND CRANES

Location. Outdoors

Players. 4 or more

Materials. A playing field with goal lines about twenty or thirty yards apart

Object. To get all players on your team

To Play. Make two teams named the Crows and the Cranes. The two teams line up in the middle of the field facing each other, an arm's length apart. The parent calls one team's name. The team that is called must turn around and run for their own goal line, and the other team chases them, trying to tag as many as possible. Players who get tagged before reaching their goal line must now join the other team. Now line up and do it again. When all players end up on one team, then start over.

Note. The parent must call each team an equal number of times but in an irregular pattern. He can increase the suspense by holding the beginning of the call: "Crrrrrrrrows!"

TAG

Location. Outdoors

Materials. None

Object. To avoid being "It"

To Play. Set boundaries and appoint one player to be "It." He chases anyone he wants, trying to tag him. Whoever he tags becomes the new "It" and play continues.

Note. Sometimes players debate over whether they really got tagged or not. If this becomes a problem, it may be wise to use flags in tag games. For flags, simply slip a strip of cloth, handkerchief, etc. through the belt in the back. "It" must have someone else's flag in his hand for a successful tag.

If one child is "It" for a long time and appears to be getting frustrated, either change the game or give him a helper.

Variations. There are many variations of Tag. Here are a few, and they can be played using any loco-motor movements.

1. Bible Tag - Play like regular tag except "It" cannot tag a player who kneels down and recites a Bible verse. "It" cannot chase that player again until he chases someone else first. Players must recite a different verse each time they are chased.

2. Dribble Tag - Play like regular tag except everyone must dribble a basketball all the time while playing.

3. Exercise Tag - Play like regular tag except "It" cannot tag a player who calls the name of an exercise and begins doing ten repetitions. "It" cannot chase that player again until he chases someone else first. Players must do a different exercise each time they are chased.

4. Frozen Tag - Anyone that "It" tags must freeze in the position he was in when he was tagged. "It" tries to freeze everyone, but if another player tags a frozen player, he thaws out and may go free.

5. Math Tag - Appoint one child to be "It." No one can move until the parent calls someone's name and then calls out a math problem. For example, "John, 3 plus 5 equals___?"

As soon as the parent says the word "equals," everyone can move. "It" chases John. Before "It" tags him, John must say, "3 plus 5 equals 8."

If John answers correctly, then everyone stops where he is, and the parent calls a new name and problem. If "It" catches John before he says the right answer, then John becomes "It."

Note. Little ones are allowed to count fingers while running.

Variations. Substitute any subject for math, using short answer questions.

6. Safety Zone Tag - Designate a safety zone such as a tree, circle on the ground, etc. "It" may not tag a player who is in the safety zone, but as soon as "It" chases someone else, the one in the safety zone must run to the far end of the boundaries.

7. Shadow Tag - "It" tries to step on someone's shadow. If he does, that person becomes "It."

8. Sign Tag - "It" displays a sign that shows that he is "It," such as holding one hand on his head. Everyone he tags must also display the sign, and they become "It" with him and help him catch other players. When everyone is caught, start over.

9. Reverse Tag - Instead of "It" trying to tag others, everyone tries to tag "It." As soon as someone tags him, that player becomes the new "It."

10. Ball Tag - "It" has the ball and tries to hit someone else with the ball as he runs. Whoever he hits becomes "It." Try this game with more than one ball so that two or more people are "It" at the same time.

Note. No hitting in the face.

CHAPTER 19

FIELD / GYM DAY

Once or twice a year it's good for home schoolers to rent a gymnasium or playing field for a support group field day or gym day. Here are a few suggestions for getting it together.

Support Group Planning. As a group, you should plan the day ahead of time. Here are a few decisions which should involve the entire group.

1. Appoint a General Overseer.
2. Select activities.
3. Appoint Activity Leaders.
4. Decide who will bring which pieces of equipment.
5. Establish a time schedule.
6. Organize the food.

General Overseer. His main responsibility is to make sure that everyone else takes care of his assigned responsibilities. He will also be the one to make announcements during the day and handle changes and emergencies. Below are a few things that need tending. The overseer doesn't have to do all these things himself, but he does need to be sure that someone takes care of them:

1. Draw up a schedule for the day, get it copied and distribute it to all parents;
2. Make necessary arrangements for gym or field rental and collect the money;
3. Secure a first-aid kit and a phone number for medical emergencies. Also, find out if anyone is allergic to bee stings;
4. Make the following announcements:
    A. Order of events
    B. Cost for rental, food, etc., and how the money will be collected; place a box at the beginning of the food table or send someone around during the meal to the head of each household to collect the money
    C. Safety rules and park/gym rules
    D. Location of phone, rest rooms, water fountains, etc.
    E. Closing time
    F. Clean-up committee
5. Make sure the place gets cleaned afterward.

Activity Leaders. Your main responsibility is to run your activity. Here are a few suggestions to help it run smoothly:

1. Secure all necessary equipment;
2. Familiarize yourself with the rules of your game or activity;
3. Bring a whistle, a watch, and don't be late;
4. Look over the playing area to be sure it is suitable;
5. Plan ahead of time how you will organize the teams. It helps to get a rough idea of how many players you will be having. Do not appoint two captains and have them pick teams. (The last ones picked always feel unwanted.) Instead, either number off or just divide the group quickly yourself;
6. Keep the competition low-key and don't be afraid to be a little flexible on the rules. Remember, this is a fun day, not a world championship;
7. Be safety conscious;
8. Report any problems to the Overseer;

Group Division. Some activities can be done with all ages together, such as tug-o-war, relay races, obstacle course, etc. Other activities, such as baseball, basketball, etc., are more enjoyable and safer if everyone is divided into general age groups. Here are a few suggested age divisions.

> Preschool - ages 2 - 5
> Elementary - ages 6 - 8
> Junior High - ages 9 - 14
> High School and up - 15 - ?

Activities. Flip through the activities section of the manual for a good variety of ideas for games, especially the Relay Races and Chase Games units.

For more ideas, check your local library for *The New Games Book* by the New Games Foundation, edited by Andrew Fleugelman.

CHAPTER 20

FOOTBALL UNIT

RELATED SKILLS

See the Basic Ball Skills unit for:

    overhand throw

    punt

    toe kick

Football Throw. Place the fingertips on the laces near one end of the ball, wrapping the thumb around. Throw with the overhand throw.

Place Kick. One player stands the ball vertically on the ground, holding it up with one finger on the top point. The holder should lean the ball slightly toward the kicker. The kicker runs up and kicks it with a toe kick.

Vocabulary

quarterback - The player who passes or kicks the ball

pass receiver - A player who runs out and tries to catch a pass

end zone - Any place beyond a team's goal line at the end of the playing field

touchdown - When a player catches a pass or punt in the other team's end zone

offense - The team that has possession of the ball

defense - The team that doesn't have possession of the ball

Games and Activities

Razzle Dazzle

Location. Outdoors

Players. 4 to 22

Materials. One or more footballs

Object. To score touchdowns

To Play. Make two teams and line each team up on their own goal line at the ends of the field. One team kicks off using a place kick. The other team (the offense) catches the ball and begins working the ball down field. All players may run at any time, but whoever is holding the ball must stop. The offense may throw or punt the ball, but no one may run with it. Encourage players to stay in the playing area, but don't stop the game just because someone steps over the boundary line. There are no organized plays and no breaks between plays; just keep moving the ball from player to player. A touchdown is scored by one player running into the other team's end zone and catching a pass or punt.

The defense may intercept a pass or punt. If so, they become the offense. If no one catches a pass or punt, then anyone may pick the ball up from the ground and play continues. If a player misses a pass or punt while in the other team's end zone, he may pick it up and pass or punt it to his own team members who are still on the playing field, and play continues.

Variation. With bigger groups, try this game with more than one ball.

PASS AND ADVANCE

Location. Outdoors

Players. 2 to 4

Materials. One football

Object. To move the ball down the length of the field with as few passes as possible or to move the ball downfield in as little time as possible (time it with a stopwatch).

To Play. Line all players up at one end of the field with one player at the other end. He kicks off from the far end using a place kick and then becomes a pass receiver. Whoever catches the kick-off becomes the quarterback. At the spot where the ball was caught, everyone runs out for a pass. The quarterback throws or punts the ball to the player of his choice. If that player catches it, he becomes the new quarterback, and play continues as above. If the ball is not caught, then everyone must return to the place where the ball was thrown. The idea is to advance the ball down the length of the field as efficiently as possible, trying not to miss any passes.

Note. Be sure everyone gets chosen to receive an equal number of passes.

PASS AND RUN

Location. Outdoors

Players. 2

Materials. One football

Object. To catch as many passes as possible

To Play. Players take turns as the quarterback and pass receiver. The receiver runs out for a pass, and the quarterback passes the ball to him. Then they switch positions. See how many passes you can catch in a row. Run different patterns when going out for passes, such as curving to the right, left, going straight ahead or running a zig-zag.

Variations. Same as above but wherever the pass receiver catches the ball, he stops there and becomes the quarterback. The other player then runs past him and goes out for a pass. Wherever he catches it, he stops, and the other player then runs past him and goes out for a pass. Play continues until the players have covered the full length of the field. Then they jog back and start over.

Try the same game but punt the ball instead of throwing it.

JOG AND PASS

Location. Outdoors

Players. 2 to 5

Materials. One football

Object. To catch as many passes as possible while running for aerobic exercise

To Play. Line players up in a straight, single-file line and have them begin jogging around the playing area, keeping fairly close together. The last player in line passes the ball to the player in front of the line. He catches it, stops and lets everyone pass him. He then passes to the new front person in line and then continues jogging in the back of the line. The one who caught the ball now stops, lets everyone pass him, then passes, and so on. This game can be done as part or all of your aerobic exercise.

Variation. Try the same game but punt the ball instead of throwing it.

OTHER GAMES USING A FOOTBALL

See the Baseball unit for:
     pickle

See the Basic Ball Skills unit for:
     back-up
     call ball
     circle pass

CHAPTER 21

FRISBEE UNIT

RELATED SKILLS

Backhand Throw. Place the right foot in front and curl the fingers of the right hand under the rim of the frisbee. Keep the index finger against the side of the rim and bend the wrist and elbow, bringing the frisbee to the left ribs. Flip the wrist and extend the arm to throw.

Skip Throw. Using a backhand throw, make the frisbee skip off the ground by throwing it downward at an angle. The left edge of the frisbee should strike the ground first about ten or twenty feet from the thrower. (This works best on pavement.)

Sandwich Catch. Sandwich the frisbee between the hands.

Two-Handed Catch. Catch it between the thumbs and fingers of both hands.

One-Handed Catch. Catch it between the thumb and fingers of one hand.

One-Finger Catch. Let the frisbee float down and catch it on one finger.

Variations. Catch or throw it behind the back or under the legs.

Games and Activities

Frisbee for Accuracy

Location. Outdoors

Players. One or more

Materials. One or more frisbees

Object. To hit the target

To Play. Designate a target and try to hit it with the frisbee from various distances. Be creative in making different types of targets. Here are a few.

> Use another player as a target and see if he can catch the frisbee without moving his feet.
> Stand an old tire upright and try to throw the frisbee through the tire.
> Make a circle with rope on the ground and try to land the frisbee in it.
> Place a bucket on the ground and try to hit it or to land the frisbee in the bucket.

Frisbee for Distance

Location. Outdoors

Players. One or more

Materials. One or more frisbees

Object. To throw the frisbee as far as possible

To Play. Designate a throwing line and see how far you can throw the frisbee. Use different throwing techniques. Here are a few.

> Stand still and throw.
> Run to the line and throw.
> Spin and throw.
> Throw with your non-dominant hand.

FRISBEE SOCCER

Location. Outdoors

Players. 4 or more

Materials. One or more frisbees

Object. To score a goal, as in soccer

To Play. Move the frisbee downfield by passing it from player to player. As soon as a player catches the frisbee, he must stop running and pass it on or shoot for a goal. No one may hold the frisbee and run with it. If you miss a pass, anyone may pick up the frisbee and pass it.

Note. Make a shooting line five or ten yards from the goal so that no one is allowed to shoot inside the line.

CHAPTER 22

GYMNASTICS UNIT

EQUIPMENT

Gymnastic mats are too expensive for most of us, but carpeted floor is sufficient for some basic tumbling skills. For extra cushioning try an additional layer of old carpet cut to a strip five or six feet wide or a layer of foam, an old mattress, etc. Gymnastics is a good activity indoors or out on the lawn.

Caution, many gymnastic activities can be somewhat dangerous for children who are not athletically inclined and/or overweight. Use discretion here and be careful not to pressure such children into attempting activities that might endanger them.

VOCABULARY

tuck - to curl the body into a tight, round ball
pike - to bend at the waist, keeping the legs straight and together
spot - to help someone perform a skill
straddle - to keep the legs straight and far apart

TUMBLING SKILLS

The skills in this unit are listed in alphabetical order. The degree of difficulty for each skill is indicated below. (This rating system is different from that used in competitive gymnastics.)

(B) - beginner
(I) - intermediate
(A) - advanced

Note. Learn beginner skills before the more difficult ones.

In all skills, the toes should be firmly pointed whenever the feet are off the floor.

Backward Roll (B). Squat down, tuck (especially the chin) and position the hands next to the ears. Roll backwards, keeping the body tucked. As the neck touches the mat, place the hands on the floor with palms down and fingers pointing toward shoulders. Pass the body over the head and land on the feet.

Spot by lifting at the hips, keeping the weight off the neck.

Variations

1. *Straddle Backward Roll (B).* Stand in a straddle position. Bend forward, reaching the hands back under the legs. Sit back, tuck the chin and begin to roll backwards, landing on the hands first. Once the bottom hits the floor, quickly place the hands next to the ears so the palms can be placed on the floor. Roll back, pulling the straddled legs over and return to a straddle stand.

Spot by lifting at the hips to keep the weight off the neck.

2. *Pike Backward Roll (I).* Stand straight and bend forward as far as possible, reaching the hands way back. Without bending the knees, sit back on the floor, letting the hands land first. The rest is the same as the backward roll but keeping in a pike position.

Spot by first holding at the shoulders and lowering the person to the floor. Then lift at the hips to keep the weight off the neck while rolling.

3. *Back Extension Roll (A).* Perform a backward roll half way until the palms are flat on the floor. In an explosive motion, push with the hands and extend the whole body straight up to a handstand.

Spot by lifting at the hips to keep the weight off the neck. Then hold the ankles.

Cartwheel (B). Mark a straight line on the floor. (Chalk works well, or lay a strip of masking tape.) Stand in a straddle with both feet on the line and the arms up straight. Moving the whole body to the right, bend the right knee and place the right hand down on the line; then the left, while lifting both legs straight up. Pass through a straddle handstand and return to straddle standing by lowering the left leg and then the right, all on the line.

Spot by holding the hips from the back. Begin with your arms crossed so that they uncross as the person goes through the cartwheel.

Variations

1. *Running Cartwheel (B)*. Run a few steps, skip and do a cartwheel. Try several cartwheels in a row.

2. *One-Arm Cartwheel (I)*. Perform a cartwheel with one arm held to your side.

Elephant Roll (B). One person lies down on his back and holds the ankles of another person who is standing at his head. The one standing bends down, holds the ankles of the other and does a forward roll, while the other stands up.

Spot by lifting at the shoulders to help stand up.

Forward Roll (B). Squat down, keeping the knees together and the chin tucked against the chest. Place the hands on the floor and roll forward to the feet while keeping the body tucked.

Spot by lifting at the hips to take the weight off the neck.

Variations

1. *Straddle Forward Roll (I)*. Stand in a straddle position and place the hands on the floor. Tuck the chin and roll forward. As you pass through a straddle sitting position, place the hands on the floor in front and push up to a straddle standing position. The legs remain straddled and straight all the way.

Spot by lifting at the shoulders to help stand up.

2. *Pike Forward Roll (A)*. Stand straight and bend forward. Keeping in a pike position, place the hands on the floor, tuck the chin and roll forward. As you pass through a sitting position, dig the heels into the mat and push on the floor with the hands. Return to standing position. (It helps to roll fast.) The knees remain straight all the way.

Spot by lifting at the shoulders to help stand up.

3. *Dive Roll (B).* Stand straight, bend the knees a little and make a very short dive into a forward roll, being *sure* to tuck the chin. Land on the hands first, then lower to the tops of the shoulders and roll. The head and neck should make very little contact with the mat. (Try a very short dive at first and dive onto an old mattress or other cushion. Gradually make the dive higher and longer. Then try it from a short run.

Spot by catching the hips and lowering down easily to keep the weight off the neck.

Kip-up (I). Roll backwards as if doing a backward roll, until the palms are flat on the floor and the hips overhead. Then stop and simultaneously and explosively whip the legs forward; push with the hands, arch the back and land on the feet.

Spot by placing your hand under the lower back as he rolls back. Then lift as he whips his legs forward to help him to his feet.

Single Leg Circles (B). Squat on one leg with the other straight out to the side. Lean on the hands and begin to swing the straight leg in a full circle, going under one hand and then the other. Try several circles in a row.

Variation

1. *Double Leg Circles (A).* Start in a push-up position with the feet straddled. Swing one foot to the other and then continue the swing with both legs together in a half circle. Then try a full circle.

2. *Log Roll (B).* Lie down with the body straight and arms overhead. Roll sideways, keeping the body straight.

3. *Round off (I).* Run a few steps, skip and do half a cartwheel. When you reach the handstand position, bring the feet together. Turn the body one quarter turn and snap the legs down. You should land facing the direction from which you came.

BALANCE AND STRENGTH SKILLS

Elbow Lever (B). Kneel down and place the palms on the floor, fingers pointing toward the knees. Bend the elbows and move them close together. Lean the lower stomach onto the elbows and balance on the hands only, holding the body straight and horizontal.

Forearm Balance (I). Place the forearms and palms on the floor with the hands close together and elbows apart, forming an inverted "V" shape. Kick the legs up straight and balance. (The head and face are supposed to stay off the floor.)

Spot by holding the ankles.

Front Scale (B). From standing, reach the arms straight out to the sides. Bend forward at the hip while lifting one leg behind and up. Balance on one straight leg with the body and other leg straight and horizontal. Look straight ahead.

Handstand (A). After mastering the Tip-up (see the next page), then try the handstand.

Stand and reach the arms straight overhead, trying to squeeze the ears with the upper arms. Place one foot in front, bend the knee and place the hands on the floor about shoulder width apart. Keep squeezing the ears and keep the elbows straight. Kick the feet up and balance with the body completely straight, feet together and head down, still squeezing the ears. It helps to push up from the shoulders, pushing the body up as high as possible. Think of trying to reach the toes to the ceiling.

Spot by holding the ankles. Try the handstand against a wall at first to get the feel of controlling your balance with your wrists and fingers.

Headstand (B). After mastering the Tripod (see the next page), then try the headstand.

Place the head and both hands on the floor to form a triangle. Kick the feet up slowly and balance with the body straight and feet together. (Roll out of the headstand by pushing up with the hands, tucking the chin and then doing a forward roll.)

Note. Most people fail at the headstand because they don't keep a triangle with the hands and head. They also kick the legs up too fast.

Spot by holding the ankles.

1. *Folded Hands Headstand (I).* Interlock the fingers and place the forearms on the floor with the elbows apart. Place the head into the cupped hands and kick up into a headstand.
2. *Crossed Arm Headstand (I).* Cross the arms and place the forearms on the floor. Place the head on the floor and kick up into a headstand.
3. *Straddle Press Headstand (I).* From a straddle stand, place the head and both hands on the floor to form a triangle. Slowly lift the legs up to a straddle headstand, then bring them together and balance.

4. *Pike Press Headstand (I)*. From a standing pike position, place the head and hands on the floor to form a triangle. Keeping the knees straight, drag the toes toward the face until all the body weight is shifted to the hands and head. Slowly lift the legs up straight and balance.

L Seat (B). Sit in a pike position. Place the hands on the floor beside the hips. Push up, holding the legs and seat off the floor with the body in the shape of an L.

Variations

1. *V Seat (A)*. Same as above, only raise the legs higher holding the body in the shape of a V.

2. *Straddle L Seat (I)*. Sit in a straddle position. Place the hands on the floor just in front of the legs. Push up, holding the legs straight, straddled, and off the floor.

3. *Pep Turn (B)*. Sit in a pike position. Place the hands behind you on the floor. Raise the hips so the body is straight. Keeping the body straight, swing one arm over and turn the body over to land in a push-up position. Then swing the other arm over and turn the body over to finish facing up with the body straight. Try several pep turns in a row.

4. *Tip-up (B)*. Squat down and place the hands on the floor with the elbows slightly bent and arms between the knees. Rest the shins just above the elbows, tip forward and balance on the hands alone. Get the feel of controlling your balance with your wrists and fingers.

Spot by holding the hips.

5. *Tripod (B)*. Place the head and hands on the floor to form a triangle. Place the knees on the elbows with the feet off the floor and balance.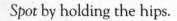

Spot by holding the hips.

PASSES AND ROUTINES

If you have space, try performing several different skills in a row; this is called a "pass." Do them one after the other, moving smoothly from one skill to the next. Here's an example of a single pass.

Straddle press headstand and forward roll out, cartwheel, front scale, half turn, back extension roll.

You can make up several different passes like this and go back and forth, one pass after another, to make a full routine.

MINI TRAMPOLINE STUNTS

Set-up. Place the mini trampoline on the floor or ground with a "crash mat" (one or two old mattresses or thick pieces of foam) just behind it. All stunts are to be done from a short run.

Basic Bounce (B). Run a few steps and land on both feet in the center of the trampoline. Bounce up as high as you can, reaching the arms up straight, keeping the body straight, feet together and toes pointed. Try to land on your feet on the crash mat.

Note. **After** mastering the "Basic Bounce," then try some other stunts. It is important to learn some basic control before going on to more difficult stunts, so don't rush into these.

Half Pirouette (B). Perform a basic bounce. After bouncing up, do a half turn while in the air. The turn is initiated by turning the head toward one shoulder. Land on the feet facing the trampoline.

Variations

1. *Full Pirouette (I).* Same as above, but do a full turn. You may need a little arm motion to help make the turn. If turning to the left, reach the right arm across the chest toward the left side, and turn the head toward the left shoulder. Land on the feet.

2. *Pike bounce (B).* Bounce up and pike, raising the legs as high as possible. Touch the finger tips to the toes while in the air. Land on the feet.

3. *Straddle Bounce (B).* Bounce up, straddle, and raise the legs as high as possible, touching the finger tips to the toes while in the air. Land on the feet.

4. *Tuck Bounce (B).* Bounce up, pull the knees up to the chest, and grab the knees with the hands. Then open and land on the feet.

5. *Dive Rolls.* These stunts must be learned in the following progression; be sure to master each step before going on to the next, to avoid injuries.

   A. Do a basic bounce and land on the feet on the mat, then do a forward roll. The hands go on the mat first, then the tops of the shoulders. The head and neck should make very little contact with the mat.
   B. Stand on the trampoline, place the hands on the crash mat and do a forward roll.
   C. Stand on the trampoline, bend way down and gently dive into a forward roll. Be very sure to tuck the chin before rolling.

D. Gradually increase the height of the dive from standing. The hands should always land first, then the tops of the shoulders. The head and neck should make very little contact with the mat. It's better to dive high and short, rather than low and long.

E. From standing on the trampoline, bounce several times and then dive into a roll. When this feels easy, go on to step F.

F. Take a short run up to the trampoline, land on both feet on the trampoline and dive into a roll. Gradually increase the height of the dive.

Note. **After** the above have been mastered and the student is able to easily dive over his own height and roll out with good control, then try some other dives.

Jack-Knife Dive (A). Bounce up high, pike and touch the toes, then straighten out as you approach the mat as if diving into water. Roll out as you land.

Swan Dive (A). Bounce up high, spread the arms wide and arch the back in mid-flight, as if soaring in the air. (Think of lifting the heels up behind you.) Then straighten out as you approach the mat and roll out.

Somersaults (flips). Do not attempt somersaults until you have had considerable experience on the trampoline. All of the other stunts should be fairly easy for you before you try these.

Front Tuck Somersault (A). (Be sure you have a good thick crash mat for this stunt.) Bounce up high while reaching straight up with the arms. Tuck into a tight ball by lifting up the hips and over the shoulders and grabbing the shins with the hands. (The shoulders are the axis of rotation.) Open up as you complete the flip but don't look at the floor. Instead, look for the wall in front of you, then land on your feet.

Front Pike Somersault (A). Same as above, only pike instead of tuck and grab the back of the thighs instead of the shins.

BALANCE BEAM

Equipment. A simple, inexpensive balance beam can be made as follows:

beam - Use a plank that is at least 1 and 1/2 inches thick, 4 to 8 inches wide, and 4 to 8 feet long.

supports - Use lumber 1 - 2 inches thick, 4 inches wide, and 2 feet long.

construction - Nail or screw the two supports to the ends of the beam. Smooth off all sharp edges and corners.

The beam can be placed on the floor for beginners. For advanced children, set it up on blocks or short stools.

BALANCE BEAM STUNTS

Beam Walk (B). Walk the length of the beam. Allow beginners to look down while walking. After they get used to it, have them look straight ahead, feeling the beam with their feet.

Variations. Try walking sideward, backward, and with the eyes closed.

After the child feels comfortable with walking, then try some other stunts.

Dip Walk (B). Stand on the left foot and bend the left knee. Lower the right foot down along the side of the beam, slide it past the left foot and bring it up in front of the left. Now try the other foot and continue for the length of the beam.

Front Scale (B). Same as the Front Scale in the tumbling section but done on the beam.

Hop (B). Hop on one foot down the length of the beam. Then try the other foot.

Jump (B). Stand on the beam and take a small jump up. Land on the beam and try to keep your balance. Gradually increase the height of the jump.

Knee Balance (B). Start on all fours on the beam. Raise one leg back, holding it straight and horizontal. Raise the arms out to the sides and balance on one knee.

L Seat (B). Sit sideways on the beam. Place the hands on the beam and push up, holding the legs up horizontally and the body in an L shape.

Spin (B). Raise up on the ball of one foot and spin on it for a half turn. Then try a full turn.

Turn (B). With both feet on the beam, raise up on the balls of the feet and swivel them 180 degrees. You should end up facing the direction you came from. Try swiveling back and forth.

V Seat (A). Same as L Seat, only raise the legs higher, holding the body in a V shape.

DISMOUNTS

Dismounting the beam means to get off it. The first dismount to try is a simple <u>jump</u> off, landing on the floor. After the jump can be done easily with control, try some others.

Cartwheel Dismount (B). Stand on the beam, so that the hands can be placed very close to the end. Kick the feet up and do a cartwheel, landing on the floor.

Dive Roll Dismount (I). Place the crash mat close to the end of the beam. Perform a dive roll off the beam into the crash mat.

Half Pirouette (B). Jump off the beam, do a half turn and land facing the beam. If that's easy, try a full pirouette.

Round-off Dismount (I). Same as a cartwheel dismount except do a round-off to the floor.

PASSES AND ROUTINES

Try performing several different balance beam skills in a row to take you smoothly from one end of the beam to the other; this is called a "pass." Do several passes moving back and forth across the length of the beam, finishing off with a dismount; this is called a routine.

VAULTING

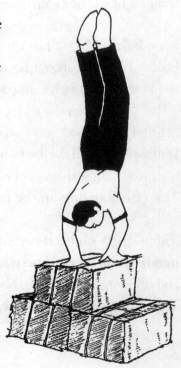

Vaulting is a fun and challenging event that is typically part of competitive gymnastics. A piece of equipment shaped somewhat like a horse's body is vaulted (leaped) over, using a variety of techniques. The height of the horse is set at about chest height. The vaulters get extra lift from a springboard which is placed a few feet in front of the horse.

For men, the vaulting horse is approached from the end. For women, the horse is approached from the side. I'd suggest using only the side approach, at least until the vaulter becomes very proficient. Be sure to master the *Beginner's Lead-Up* before attempting any other vaults; then take them in the order they are presented below, from least to most difficult.

Equipment. As an inexpensive substitute for a vaulting horse, set up three bales of hay in a pyramid. (Inquire at your nearest farm stand or Agway Farm Supply store where to purchase hay bales.) You may also want to put an old mattress on the ground for a landing pad.

Most of us don't have access to a springboard, but a mini trampoline will serve the same purpose. For beginners, place the trampoline six inches to a foot in front of the horse. As students progress, the trampoline should be moved further back, as much as several feet, but only as the vaulter feels comfortable with the distance.

Even if you don't have a mini trampoline, most children can still perform many of the vaults given here by jumping directly off the ground.

Caution. Vaulting can be somewhat dangerous for children who are not athletically inclined and/or are overweight. Use discretion here and be careful not to pressure such children into attempting vaults that might endanger them.

Beginner Vaults

Beginner's Lead-up. Stand on the ground with the hands resting on the top of the vault horse (hay bale). Jump up while pushing down with the hands and land on both knees on top of the horse. Then hop off. Practice this until it is easy to do, then go on to the Squat Vault.

> NOTE: Except where otherwise mentioned, in all following vaults the hands are the only body parts that touch the horse. The vaulter should attempt to raise his hips as much as possible before the body passes over the horse, as this makes each vault easier.

> CAUTION: On every vault be sure to bend the knees on the landing to absorb the weight of the body. Never land stiff-legged, as that could cause injury.

Spotting. Spot all vaults as much as necessary by standing close to the horse on the side of the landing area. Catch the vaulter by reaching one arm across the chest and the other arm across the back. The idea is to help the vaulter to land on his feet with control.

Squat Vault. Take a short run up to the vaulting horse and jump with a two foot take-off. Place both hands on the horse, keep the elbows straight, and bend the knees pulling them up toward the chest and allowing them to pass between the arms. The body passes over the horse in a squatting position. Then try to land on both feet with control.

Note: Beginners will often stumble somewhat during the landing, but, ideally, there should be no additional steps once the feet land on the ground. The proficient vaulter bends his knees on the landing to absorb his body weight, then resumes a straight standing position with arms raised straight overhead to demonstrate that he has complete control of his body.

Straddle Vault. Take a short run up to the vaulting horse and jump with a two-foot take-off. Place both hands on the horse, keep the elbows straight and straddle the legs as wide as possible. The body passes over the horse with the legs straddled, knees straight and toes pointed. Then try to land on both feet with control.

Thief Vault. Take a short run up to the vaulting horse and jump with a two-foot take-off. Place both hands on the horse, keep the elbows straight, bend the knees somewhat and allow them to pass around the outside of the arms to one side. The body passes over the horse in a squatting position, but over one end of the horse, rather than between the arms. Then try to land on both feet with control.

Intermediate Vaults

Note: These vaults should only be attempted after the Beginner Vaults can be performed easily with good control. The vaulter should be able to perform the beginner vaults with his hips raised to about shoulder height as he passes over the horse. Intermediate Vaults require a bit more speed, so lengthen the run up to the horse. The point of take-off should be moved further back from the horse to allow more time for the hips to rise.

Stoop Vault. Take a longer run up to the vaulting horse and jump with a two-foot take-off. The remainder of this vault is exactly the same as the Squat Vault except the knees are kept straight as the body passes between the arms. The hips must be elevated at least as high as the shoulders during this vault. Then try to land on both feet with control. Of course, the knees bend on the landing to absorb the weight of the body.

Cartwheel Vault. (Only for vaulters who can already perform a cartwheel easily on the ground.) Take a longer run up to the vaulting horse and jump with a two-foot take-off. Place the hands apart, one in front of the other, as in a ground cartwheel. The hips and legs are raised high overhead with the body passing through a handstand position with the legs straddled. The body is facing one side as it passes over the horse. On the way down, the feet come together, and the vaulter lands on both feet, standing sideways to the horse.

Round-off Vault. (only for vaulters who can already perform a round-off easily on the ground) Take a longer run up to the vaulting horse and jump with a two-foot take-off. The hands are placed apart, one in front of the other. The vaulter raises his whole body up overhead and passes through a handstand position. The arms and legs are straight, and the legs are together with the toes pointed. The body faces one side as it passes over the horse, but on the way down the vaulter turns one quarter turn and lands facing the horse on both feet.

Headspring Vault. (Only for vaulters who can already perform a headspring easily on the ground.) Take a longer run up to the vaulting horse and jump with a two-foot take-off. Place the hands and head on the horse, forming a triangle as in a headstand. The hips rise high overhead while the body assumes a pike position. As the hips pass over the horse, the vaulter springs explosively out of the pike position into the arched position, whipping the legs over quickly and pushing off the horse with the arms. Before, landing the vaulter straightens his body and lands as usual with the feet together.

CHAPTER 23

HAND - EYE COORDINATION UNIT

SKILLS

Balancing a Stick. Place a stick vertically in the palm of the hand and balance it. Use a broom stick, baseball bat, dowel, etc.

Variations. Try balancing the stick on one finger, the head, chin, nose, shoulder, knee or foot.

Try other objects to balance, such as a small stool, chair, etc. The key to balancing anything is to put the center of gravity over the point of balance.

Toss and Catch a Stick. Toss the stick up and catch it. If that's easy, try doing a half flip and catch. Try a full flip, then a double flip. Try passing it to another player, first with no flip, then half, etc.

Juggling. (Use tennis balls, bean bags, etc.) Start with one ball, tossing it up with one hand and catching it with the other. The key to juggling is to toss the balls consistently at the same height and following the same arch every time. When you get pretty consistent, try two balls, using both hands.

Juggling Two Balls. Hold one ball in each hand, toss one up, then the other, then catch them in the opposite hands.

Another way is to *toss* with only the right hand and *catch* with only the left. Each time the left hand catches a ball, quickly place it in the right hand and toss it. The balls travel in a circular motion.

Try juggling two balls, using one hand, tossing them straight up.

Juggling Three Balls. Hold two balls in the right hand and one in the left. Toss right, left, right, etc., catching in the opposite hands.

Another way is to *toss* with only the right hand and *catch* with only the left. Each time the left hand catches a ball, quickly place it in the right hand and toss it. The balls travel in a circular motion.

Two-Player Juggling. Start by passing one ball back and forth. Then pass two balls, passing at the same time. Then try three balls, keeping one in the air all the time.

OTHER ACTIVITIES

See the Basic Ball Skills unit for other skills that develop hand/eye coordination:

    throwing skills
    catching skills
    dribbling skills
    passing skills

CHAPTER 24

HANDBALL UNIT

Equipment. Use any small ball that is fairly soft, such as a tennis ball. The ball is hit with the open palm, so you may want to wear gloves if it hurts your hand.

RELATED SKILLS

Players should always keep their eyes on the ball while hitting it and follow through with the stroke.

Forehand Stroke. Turn sideways with the left shoulder toward the target, knees slightly bent, feet shoulder width or more. Swing the right arm level, keeping the elbow slightly bent, wrist firm and hand cupped. Lean into the stroke as contact is made.

Cross-over Stroke. Turn sideways with the right shoulder toward the target, knees slightly bent, and feet shoulder width or more. Cross the right arm over to the left side, bending the elbow. Turn the right hand so the palm faces forward and hit the ball.

Underhand Stroke. Face the target and hit the ball straight ahead while lunging forward on the left foot.

Overhead Stroke. Face the target and hit the ball straight ahead while lunging forward on the left foot.

Serving. Beginners should use a forehand stroke to serve. First bounce the ball, then hit it on the bounce.

Practice. For individual practice of skills, you can hit the ball against a wall. For practice in pairs, hit the ball back and forth, letting it bounce about midway between the players.

GAMES AND ACTIVITIES

HANDBALL

Location. In or outdoors

Players. 1 or 2

Materials. One small ball

Object. To hit the ball back and forth as many times as possible

To Play. Players stand several yards apart and hit the ball to each other, making it bounce one time in the middle.

Variations. Play individually by hitting the ball against a wall. Play with two players, taking turns hitting it against the wall.

FOUR SQUARE BALL

Location. In or outdoors

Players. 2 to 4

Materials. One ball, big or small

Object. To hit the ball as many times as possible

To Play. Mark a square on the floor or ground about ten feet by ten feet. Divide it into four squares and assign one player to a square. Players hit the ball with open hands to one another on one bounce. See how many hits you can get in a row without letting the ball go out of the big square.

CHAPTER 25

LOCOMOTOR SKILL UNIT

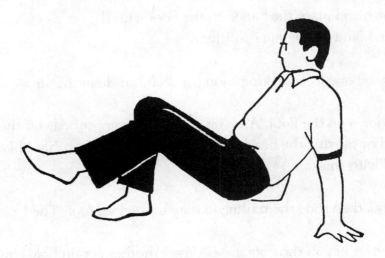

There are many different ways to move the body through space; these are called locomotor skills. They are fun and challenging, they contribute to physical fitness, and they help the child gain body awareness, agility and control. For beginners, these skills should first be learned and practiced all by themselves. When the skills have been mastered, they can be incorporated into various games and activities.

COMMON LOCOMOTOR SKILLS

walk
run
crawl
skip
gallop
one-foot hop
two-foot hop

Try these skills moving forward, backward and sideward.

Less Common Locomotor Skills

Crab Walk - Sit on the floor with knees bent. Place the hands on the floor behind the hips and hold the body up on the hands and feet. Walk like a crab by moving the hands and feet.

Cross-over Step - Run sideways, crossing the legs with each step.

Frog Hop - Squat down and place the hands on the floor with the arms between the knees. Spring forward like a frog and land in the same position.

Leap - Run and jump off one foot, making a long, graceful stride in the air.

Seal Walk - Lie face down on the floor. Arch up, holding the upper body off the floor with the hands. Walk forward by moving the hands only. The legs must drag behind like a seal. (Sound effects are permitted with this one.)

Shuffle - Step sideways, then slide the trailing foot up to the lead foot. The legs don't cross.

Wheelbarrel - One person lies on the floor, face down. Another person holds his ankles like a wheel barrel. The one on the floor pushes up and walks on his hands.

Gymnastics Skills - See the Gymnastics Unit for the following skills which can be used as locomotor skills:

> log roll
> forward rolls
> backward rolls
> cartwheel
> round off
> handstand (walk on hands)

GAMES AND ACTIVITIES

LEAP FROG

Location. In or outdoors

Players. 2 or more

Materials. None

Object. To hop over all the players

To Play. Players kneel on the floor in a straight row, crouched up in a tight ball. All players face front, keeping about one or two feet between them. The last player then does a frog hop over each player, placing his hands on each player's back as he hops over. He continues to hop until he reaches the front. As soon as a player becomes the last one in the line, he goes; he does not wait for the one in front of him to finish.

When everyone has had a turn to hop, start over.

Variation

High Leap Frog. Same as above, but instead of crouching on the floor, players stand in line several feet apart, bend over and place their hands on their knees. The hopper takes a short run, places his hands on each player's back and straddles his legs as he hops over.

FOLLOW THE LEADER

Location. In or outdoors

Players. 2 or more

Materials. None

Object. To move from one place to another, the same way the leader does

To Play. Mark off a starting point and a finishing point. (It can be a straight line, or around obstacles.) Select a leader who uses any locomotor skill he chooses to travel from the starting point to the finish. Other players follow along the same way and take turns being the leader.

Other Uses

Use various locomotor skills for relay races, chase games or for a different way to run the bases in baseball, etc. They can also be used as a handicap in games by requiring an advanced child to travel by a more difficult locomotor skill. This provides much more opportunity for beginners and advanced players to play together.

CHAPTER 26

OBSTACLE COURSE UNIT

In or outdoors, set up a series of obstacles that the players need to overcome. Players may run the course either individually, or they may help one another in pairs, groups, or as one big group. Here are a few examples of obstacles.

1. Walk across a balance beam or a picnic table bench.

2. Stand an old tire upright to climb through.

3. Hang a rope from a tree and require each player to swing over an area of ground.

4. Place both feet in a sack and hop from one obstacle to the next.

5. Lay a stepladder on the ground and require each player to step on each rung with both feet and both hands.

6. Hurdle (jump) over several objects while running from one obstacle to another. Use objects, such as laundry baskets, five gallon pails, cardboard boxes, etc.

7. Hop on one foot (or do any other locomotor skill) to a small rug and do ten repetitions of an exercise, such as sit-ups or push-ups.

8. Climb over one sawhorse and under another.

9. Balance a book or beanbag on your head while going from one obstacle to the next.

10. Run up and down a set of stairs.

11. Swing from a rope in a tree over an obstacle.

12. Stretch a big rope about three feet high, between two trees and travel the length of the rope while holding with the hands and legs.

13. Fix (securely) a ladder horizontally at about head height and have players swing from rung to rung down the length of the ladder.

14. Go up a slide instead of down and walk down the ladder.

15. Spoon brigade - Place a bucket of water about ten yards away from an empty cup. Each player gets a teaspoon to carry water to the cup. When the cup runs over, the course is finished.

Variation. Skip the spoon brigade and have each player run the whole course carrying a cup of water. As players finish the course, have them pour their water into a quart container. The players must continue running the course and carrying more cups of water until the container runs over.

Many local parks have a great assortment of playground equipment that you could easily use for running an obstacle course. Try playing follow the leader, letting each child lead the rest through a course of his own design.

CHAPTER 27

PADDLEBALL / RACQUETBALL UNIT

These two activities are combined since they involve the same basic skills and games.

Indoor Materials. One small nerf ball for every two players and a paddle or short-handled racquet for each player. Paddles can be anything, such as ping pong paddles, small cutting boards, or even family rods of correction.

Outdoor Materials. Same as above, but any small ball will do, such as a tennis ball.

Related Skills

In practice and games, players should always keep their eyes on the ball while hitting it and follow through with the stroke.

Skills can be practiced individually by hitting the ball against a wall. Pairs can practice by taking turns hitting it against a wall or hitting it back and forth.

Forehand Stroke. Turn sideways with the left shoulder toward the target, knees slightly bent, feet shoulder width or more. Swing the right arm level, keeping the elbow slightly bent and wrist firm. Lean into the stroke as contact is made.

Backhand Stroke. Turn sideways with the right shoulder toward the target, knees slightly bent and feet shoulder width or more. Swing the right arm level, keeping the elbow slightly bent and wrist firm. Lean into the stroke as contact is made.

Underhand Stroke. Face the target and hit the ball straight ahead while lunging forward on the left foot.

Overhead Stroke. Face the target and hit the ball straight ahead while lunging forward on the left foot.

Serving. Beginners should use a forehand or underhand stroke to serve. First bounce the ball, then hit it on the bounce.

Games and Activities

Paddleball / Racquetball

Location. In or outdoors

Players. 1 or more

To Play. Same as handball
(See the Handball unit.)

CHAPTER 28

PILLOW POLO UNIT

RELATED SKILLS

There are no special skills needed for this game; just hit the ball and have fun.

PILLOW POLO

Location. In or outdoors

Players. 2 or more

Materials. A pillow for each player or you can substitute a piece of foam pipe insulation or a foam covered bat (available at some department stores). You can also send away to Flaghouse Inc. for an official pillow polo set (see the Equipment section of the manual).

You also need one or more nerf balls (any size). Balloons can be used indoors.

Object. To score goals

To Play. Make two teams and have a goal at each end of the playing area. As in soccer or hockey, players work the ball to the other team's goal and try to score. The ball can only be hit with pillows that are held in the hands (no kicking).

CHAPTER 29

PING PONG UNIT

This game can be practiced and played on any table, but big tables are better.

RELATED SKILLS

Forehand Stroke. (For a ball coming on the right side.) Stand with the left shoulder slightly angled toward the table. Swing the right arm a short way and snap the wrist just a little to hit the ball.

Backhand Stroke. (For a ball coming in front or on the left side.) Stand with the right shoulder angled slightly toward the table. Move the right hand in front of the body or cross it over to the left side, keeping the palm toward yourself. Extend the arm out straight to hit the ball backhanded.

Serve. Bounce the ball on the table and hit it with either a forehand or backhand stroke. Another way is to hit the ball out of the hand with either stroke. A serve must always hit the server's side of the table before going over the net.

GAMES AND ACTIVITIES

PING PONG

Location. In or outdoors.

Players. 2 to 4

Materials. One paddle for each player, a table, ping pong balls, net (optional).

Object. To volley back and forth as many times as possible

To Play. One side serves the ball, and players try to continue hitting it back and forth. Each time the ball is hit, it must bounce only once on the side of those receiving the serve. Receivers may hit the ball before it bounces on their side. If the ball is missed, whoever picks it up may serve to start over. See how many volleys in a row you can achieve.

Variation. This game can be played with one player if you move the table against a wall. The player hits the ball against the wall and lets it bounce back off the wall.

Note: It takes a while for beginners to get the hang of this game, so loosen up on the rules for them. Keep trying to volley back and forth even if the ball hits the floor, ceiling, wall or bounces more than once on one player's side. No matter what happens, as long as they can return the ball, let them keep adding the volleys to their score. As they improve their skills, gradually stiffen up on the rules to keep it challenging. When they get really proficient, try narrowing the boundaries of the table for added challenge, or play left-handed. For an exciting challenge, see how many times players can volley back and forth in one minute.

ROUND TABLE

Location. In or outdoors.

Players. 3 to 8

Materials. One paddle for each player, a table, a ping pong ball, a net(optional)

Object. To volley the ball back and forth as many times as possible

To Play. Players form a circle around the table. One player serves and the whole group moves around the table one position. The player at the non-serving end of the table returns the ball, and everyone rotates again one position. The challenge is to keep the ball volleying back and forth while the whole group runs around the table with each player taking his turn to hit the ball.

CHAPTER 30

RELAY RACES UNIT

Relay races can be held in or outdoors with two or more people. Here are a few hints at running relays.

SET-UP

```
X     X
X     X          teams
X     X
X     X
X     X          starting line
_____


_____
            turn-around line
```

Organizational Hints

1. Use marks on the ground, a rope, garden hose, stick, bucket, etc. to designate starting and turn-around lines.

2. Make the distance to the turn-around line appropriate for the skill being performed. (You can run a lot farther than you can hop on one foot.)

3. To start, players *stand* in line behind the starting line, run to the turn-around line, turn around and return to the starting line where they tag the hand of the next player in line. The next player must wait to be tagged before he goes.

4. Players who have finished their turn must <u>sit</u> in line. This prevents confusion and helps everyone to know which players have already had their turn.

5. If you have only two or three players, you can still run a relay race. Make one team of the players and time them. Run the race several times to see if they can beat their score.

6. With bigger groups, make several teams and make the teams small enough so that players don't have to wait a long time for their turn.

7. Allow older players to help younger ones with difficult skills.

8. If you have more than one team, keep the competition low-key by instructing those who are finished to encourage those who are still running, regardless of whose team they're on. And when everyone is finished, don't make a spectacle of the team that finished first, just go on to the next race.

Relay Races

Balance Race. Players must run back and forth while balancing an object on their heads, such as a beanbag, book, etc.

Balloon Pop Race. Place a chair for each team at the turn-around line. Give each player a balloon that is blown up and tied. Players run to the chair, sit on the balloon to pop it and return.

Dribbling Race. Players run while performing various dribbling skills. (See the Basic Ball Skills Unit for dribbling skills.)

Hot Air Races. Players demonstrate who has the most hot air by blowing a cotton ball, balloon or feather across the floor. (Make this one short.)

Jump Rope Race. Each player must travel back and forth while jumping rope.

Locomotor Skill Race. Most of the skills in the Locomotor Skills Unit of the manual are suitable for relay races.

Over and Under Race. Players stand in straight lines with about two feet between each player. Give the first player of each team a ball. He passes it over his head to the second player who passes it under his legs to the third. The team continues passing it, over, then under, to the end of the line. When the last player gets the ball, he runs to the front of the line and begins it again. Continue until each player has been first in his line.

Pass and Sit Race. Teams stand in straight lines with the leader facing his team. He passes the ball to the second player who catches it, throws it back and sits. The leader catches it and throws it to the next player who catches it, throws it back, and sits, etc. When everyone is sitting, you're finished. Use various throwing skills from the Basic Ball Skills Unit.

Passing Relay Race. Players run in pairs, passing a ball back and forth as they run. Use the chest pass or bounce pass. (See the Basic Ball Skills Unit for throwing skills.)

Quick Change Race. Give each team a set of extra-large clothes (hat, overcoat, gloves, boots, etc.). Players must carry the clothes to the turn-around line, put the clothes on, run to the finish line and remove the clothes. Then the next player goes.

Sack Race. Players place both feet into a grain sack, pull it up to their waists, and hop back and forth.

Three-Legged Race. Two players go together, each putting one foot into the same grain sack.

CHAPTER 31

SOCCER UNIT

RELATED SKILLS

See the Basic Ball Skills Unit for: kicking skills and miscellaneous skills.

The following skills are called "foot traps"; they are for stopping a ball that is rolling to you. The idea is to stop the ball dead at your feet, not letting it bounce away.

Sole of the Foot Trap. As the ball rolls to you, place the sole (bottom) of the foot on top of the ball and trap it between your foot and the ground.

Inside or Outside of the Foot Trap. Turn the foot sideways (either way) and hold it several inches above the ground. Allow the ball to hit the foot and let the foot move backwards to absorb the force. (This takes some practice to master.)

Shin Trap. Stand in front of the oncoming ball. Bend both knees over the ball and allow it to hit the shins.

Games and Activities

Soccer

Location. Outdoors

Players. 4 or more

Materials. One soccer ball and two goals

Object. To score goals

To Play. Set boundaries around your yard; make a goal about ten feet wide at either end of the playing area. Draw or mark a goalie's circle arching about ten feet in front of each goal. (You can use a rope or garden hose placed in a semi-circle to form the goalie's circle.)

Make two teams. Half of each team will play the offense, and the other half will play the defense.

The job of the offense is to score goals. They generally stay on the far end of the field, but they may come back to help the defense.

The job of the defense is to prevent the other team from scoring. Defensive players may go on the other half of the field but will generally stay on their own half, always trying to work the ball up to their own offensive players.

The ball may be kicked or bounced off any body parts except the arms and hands. If someone hits the ball with the arms or hands, even by accident, it is called "hands," and the other team gets a free shot from wherever it happened. Only the goalie may try to stop a free shot.

The goalie remains in the goal most of the time. He may kick the ball or use his hands to catch and throw the ball, as long as he is in the goalie's circle. Once he comes out of the goalie's circle, he must play like everyone else. With small groups the goalie should come out of the goalie's circle more often to play defense. With very small groups, it may be better to have no goalie at all.

To start the game, line up the offensive players from both teams, facing each other on the midline of the field. Defensive players stay back, being spread out around their half of the field. Give the ball to one team; as soon as they touch the ball, play begins and continues until someone scores, or the ball goes out of bounds. If someone scores, start again as above, giving the ball to the team that did not score. If the ball goes out of bounds, whoever touched it last is held responsible, and someone on the other team throws it in. The throw-in must be done using a two-handed throw, with the ball passing over the top of the head and feet remaining on the ground.

MULTI-BALL SOCCER

Location. Outdoors

Players. 1 or more

Materials. At least one ball for every player (extra balls are even better)

Object. To score a goal and help someone else

To Play. Line the balls along the midline of the field. Each player dribbles a ball with his feet across the field and shoots at the goal. There are no goalies. Once a player scores a goal, the ball stays in the net, and he goes to get another ball. If there are no balls left, then he helps another player score a goal, but he may not take a ball away from someone else.

Note. You may want to make a line or half circle ten or twenty feet or more in front of each goal to be the shooting line. Without this line, players will typically dribble right up to the goal and never practice their shooting.

Variations

1. This game can be played with teams or individually.

2. Play indoors with nerf balls or balloons.

3. Try timing the group to see how fast they can shoot all the balls in the goal.

4. Try requiring different kinds of kicks to be used when shooting.

CRAB SOCCER

Location. In or outdoors

Players. 2 or more

Materials. One or more soccer or nerf balls

Object. To score goals

To Play. Played like regular soccer, but all players must stay in the "crab walk" position throughout the game. (See "crab walk" in the Locomotor Skills Unit of the manual.)

SPEEDBALL

Location. Outdoors

Materials. One ball

Object. To score a goal as in soccer

To Play. This game incorporates various skills from basketball, volleyball, football and soccer. There is no "out of bounds," and the ball may be moved downfield from player to player and shot at the goal by any type of throwing, kicking, dribbling or volleying. You may also pass to yourself by throwing the ball ahead of you, running under it and catching it yourself. There are only two things you may not do:

1. You may not carry the ball and run with it (as in football).
2. You may not pick the ball up off the ground with your hands.

You may, however, kick the ball up with your foot to another player who can catch it in his hands, or you may lift it to yourself, using one or both feet and then catch it in your hands.

Variations. Try more than one ball.

Chapter 32

Swimming Unit

Swimming is an excellent all-around exercise that works most muscle groups and can provide the aerobic effect as well. It's a good activity for the summer physical education program because we often don't feel like doing most other activities when it's hot.

Where to Swim

We can swim wherever there is reasonably clean water, such as the ocean, lake, pond, river, creek or pool. However, as Christians we need to be very careful about modesty, both of ourselves and of others. A typical public beach or pool with nearly-naked sunbathers lying around is no place for any Christian. We need a private swimming area that is fenced in. If we don't have access to such a place, then it may be better not to include swimming in the physical education program.

A Homemade Pool

A simple, homemade pool can be built for about $150.00, and a small filter will cost about $100.00 more.

You could make such a pool any size you like, but we have had success with a pool that is five feet wide, ten feet long, and two feet deep; big enough for anyone to learn most of the basic skills of swimming. The sides are framed with two by fours, and faced off with half-inch plywood; all lumber is pressure treated. The pool has no bottom but sits on the ground with a sheet of roofing rubber as a liner, held up by strips of one inch by two inch lumber around the inside perimeter.

Visit your local lumberyard and roofing supplies store for materials.

Learning To Swim

Learning to swim is best accomplished by following a step-by-step procedure. The earliest steps are most important for overcoming the fear of the water. If these steps are rushed or skipped, it makes all the rest very difficult, if not impossible. So take your time and allow your children to move from step to step as they are ready. It's one thing to *encourage* them to move on, it's quite another to <u>force</u> them. Never throw a child into the water or push someone's face in. Give non-swimmers (of any age) plenty of time to experiment in the water with each step, repeating it many times until they feel comfortable with it. As you move from step to step, be sure to review and practice previous steps regularly.

Safety

Water safety is basically common sense:

- no diving into shallow water
- always have responsible supervision
- no pushing, etc.

WHAT TO WEAR

If our swimming area is completely fenced in, then we can wear whatever we want, as long as brothers and sisters have separate swimming times. If the whole family must all swim together, then we should wear something modest: modern swimsuits, or wet T-shirts and shorts are not modest. Something, such as one-piece culottes outfit for girls, and pants and short-sleeve shirt for boys, would be proper (in the author's opinion).

GETTING USED TO THE WATER

Non-swimmers of any age need to go through this step. It may take anywhere from a few minutes to a few years for someone to feel relaxed in the water. No one should move on to later steps until he feels comfortable in the water.

A child is never too young to get used to the water. Infants and toddlers do well in a warm bath tub, just splashing around and playing with toys. Here are a few other activities to help young children get used to pool, pond or lake water.

- Have the child walk around in knee-deep water, then sit in it.

- Sit on the edge of a pool and splash the feet.

- Play with toys in shallow water.

- Hug the child closely and slowly inch him into the water with you. Move around while hugging him and eventually hold him away from your body, moving him around on his stomach, back and sides.

- Once a person is used to the water, try walking on all fours. Then lie on the stomach and walk on the hands like a seal; add kicking the feet.

For each new step or skill, it's a good idea for the parent to be right there in the water. Explain and demonstrate the skill and carry the child through it until he feels confident that he can do it himself. Be patient.

GETTING THE FACE WET

Once someone feels comfortable in the water, he needs to learn to get his face wet without having a panic attack. Here are some suggestions to help.

- Rub your own wet hands on your face. (See, it doesn't hurt at all.)

- In still water, lower the chin under, then the mouth.

- Pinch the nose and lower it into the water, still keeping the eyes out.

- With the mouth and nose under, try blowing bubbles with the mouth, then the nose.

- Try to hold your breath and count to ten.

- Try to say something underwater.

- Now close the eyes, pinch the nose, and put the whole face in, eyes and all.

- Hold your breath, blow bubbles and talk.

- Next, go for the whole head, repeating as above.

Floating

Once a child knows that he can float, he'll soon be swimming.

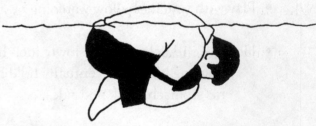

Tuck Float. In shallow water, hold your breath, put your face in the water (hold your nose if you want), tuck up in a tight ball, stay still and float face down as long as you can.

Dead Man's Float. Start in a tuck float, then reach the arms overhead and outward to form a Y shape with the body. Next, straighten the legs out and float.

Back Float. This is more difficult, especially for those who have very little body fat. In shallow water, lie on your back, arch your back (think about pushing your belly up), reach the arms out to the sides and overhead to form a Y, and keep breathing normally. Parents should help the child into this position, supporting him at first, then gradually giving less support. See if you can stay up without moving. If not, try kicking a bit; this will keep the feet up. You can also use the hands to keep you up by sculling (see the Sculling section below).

FLUTTER KICK

This exercise can be done in shallow water while lying on the stomach with the hands on the bottom. It can also be done while holding the edge of a pool with both hands.

While lying on the stomach, kick the feet alternately up and down in a short, quick, fluttering motion, keeping the toes pointed. It's OK to splash a little but try to keep the feet under the surface most of the time.

Practice using the flutter kick to move through the water by lying on an air mattress, wearing a lifevest or holding any kickboard or flotation device with the hands. Try it on your back.

Homemade Kickboard. You can make a kickboard out of foam insulation or a pine board. Make it about two inches thick, ten inches wide, and twenty inches long. Cut one end round and sand all edges and corners.

GLIDING

In shallow water, place the face in the water, reach both arms straight in front (think of squeezing the ears with the upper arms) and push off with the feet. Glide as far as you can. In a pool, you can push off from the side.

When this is easy, try to keep yourself going by adding the flutter kick.

Try gliding on your back.

DOGGIE PADDLE

Squat down in shallow water, walk along the bottom and move the arms alternately in a circular motion in front, as if pedaling a bicycle with the hands. This helps the child to feel that he can pull himself along with his hands in the water. Think of reaching out and pulling the water to the belly. Now try this with the face in the water.

Gradually have the child push off and glide a little with the face in the water and paddle with the hands. The hands and wrists are flat and straight. Eventually, add the flutter kick.

Progress to doing the doggie paddle completely underwater. Then try it with the head above the water.

Encourage children to try to reach the arms farther in front all the time. At first, their strokes will be short and fast. Eventually, you want them to reach the arms straight in front for long, smooth, rhythmic strokes.

Sculling

Get on all fours in shallow water. Lean back on the legs enough to hold yourself up. Place the hands in the water with the palms facing down. Tilt the thumbs downward and move the hands apart a short way. Then tilt the thumbs up and move the hands together. Repeat this arm and hand motion quickly and feel how it tends to push you up. This is sculling.

Now lean forward, lie on your stomach and see if you can hold your upper body up and your head out of the water by sculling. If so, straighten the knees so that only the feet are touching the bottom.

Next, try sculling while doing the flutter kick. When that's easy, try it on your back. Glide first, then scull with your hands at your sides. First try it with the flutter kick, then without kicking.

Bobbing

This is a lead-up skill for rhythmic breathing. Practice it in the following progression:

1. Close the eyes, pinch the nose, dunk the whole head under and come right up.

2. Try it twice in a row.

3. Bob up and down five or ten times in a row (at your own pace), taking a fresh breath each time you come up.

4. Dunk under once, blow out all your air and come up.

5. Dunk under, blow out your air, come up, take a quick breath, go back under, exhale and come up.

6. Work up to ten bobs, each time blowing the air out before coming up. Try to time it so that you run out of air just before you come up. Then take one quick breath while you're up and go back under. You should be under water much longer than above during this step.

7. Try bobbing without pinching the nose. If you blow out through your nose as you go down, it will keep water out of your nose.

8. When you can bob for two or three minutes without stopping, always exhaling while under and inhaling while up, then you're ready to move on.

RHYTHMIC BREATHING

This is one of the most important and difficult skills to learn. It will take a while to master, so be patient. Practice it first out of the water; then when you have the idea, try it in the water.

This exercise can be done in shallow water while kneeling or lying on the stomach with the hands on the bottom. Learn it in the following progression.

1. Place the face just above the water, turn the head to the right side, open the mouth wide and take a breath, place the face in the water and come back up. Do it several times.

2. Repeat as above but this time blow out mostly through the nose and a little through the mouth while the face is in the water, then lift the head out.

3. Try this again but this time keep exhaling with the face in the water until you run out of air; then lift the head out.

4. Do this ten or twenty times until it feels fairly comfortable to exhale underwater. Be sure to empty the lungs before lifting the head out. There is no holding of the breath.

5. Now try it again but this time don't <u>lift</u> the head out when you run out of air. Instead, keep the head in the water and <u>roll</u> it to the right side. The left ear and back of the head stay underwater while the face is turned out to inhale. The head never comes completely out of the water. After inhaling, immediately begin exhaling and roll the face back into the water.

6. Try two, then three, then four repetitions in a row without taking the head completely out of the water.

7. Keep adding to the number of repetitions, until the person can keep inhaling and exhaling rhythmically for two or three minutes. He must be fairly relaxed while doing so, never holding the breath.

8. Next, hold the edge of the pool or a flotation device, and do the flutter kick while breathing rhythmically.

9. When you can breath and kick continuously for two or three minutes, try the doggie paddle using rhythmic breathing.

Strokes

All strokes should be practiced first on dry land to get the idea. Then kneel or stand in shallow water or have the parent hold and support the child.

Crawl Stroke

To Start. Glide with the face in the water. Begin the flutter kick, keeping the arms straight in front.

The Stroke. Press the right arm down, pull toward the feet, then push toward the feet. Keep the elbow slightly bent, hand and wrist straight and flat and positioned directly under the midline of the body. As the right hand passes under the hips, lift the arm completely out of the water. Do not lift the arm straight up through a vertical plane but bring it around more horizontally, keeping it fairly close to the water's surface, with the elbow straight. While returning the right arm to the glide position straight in front, repeat the stroke with the left arm; press the left arm down, pull toward the feet, then push toward the feet, as above. Be sure to lift the left arm completely out of the water when the stroke is finished. The arms alternate rhythmically.

Practice the stroke many times while swimming short distances, holding your breath with your face in the water. When you can do it properly, go on to breathing.

Breathing. Beginning swimmers are usually taught to breathe only on the right side, just to avoid confusion. The right side will be explained here, but some swimmers prefer to breathe on the left instead; either way is fine.

After you can do the crawl stroke well with your face in the water, then try it while holding the face out of the water. Let the face follow each arm as it travels in the air but inhale only on the right side. After inhaling, immediately begin exhaling and continue as the face moves to the left side and back to the right. You should run out of air just as the right arm is finishing its stroke.

Practice this until you can swim smoothly for several minutes, breathing continuously with the face out of the water.

Rhythmic Breathing. Kneel or stand in shallow water to practice this.

Begin the arm motions as above but after taking a breath, immediately begin exhaling as you roll the face into the water for one-quarter turn. The face points straight down, and the breath is never held. As the right arm nears the completion of the stroke, and you begin lifting it out of the water, *roll* (don't lift) the head to the right. The mouth and face come out of the water, but the left ear and back of the head stay in. Take a breath and return the face to the water as the right arm re-enters the water. Think of following the right arm with the face; they are always in or out of the water together.

Once you have the idea while kneeling, then practice swimming this way until it feels comfortable.

Later, try breathing on every other right arm stroke.

BREAST STROKE

Arm Stroke. Perform a glide with the face out of the water. As the glide loses its momentum, rotate the arms so that the palms face outward. With the wrists and elbows straight, move the arms apart in a horizontal plane until the hands are about in line with the lower ribs (approximately 100 degrees). Now bend the elbows and bring the hands together as if praying and reach in front again. Repeat, making circular motions with the hands.

Frog Kick. The breast stroke uses the frog kick. This skill can be learned while holding the edge of a pool or in shallow water, keeping the hands on the bottom.

Draw the knees up and apart, keeping the feet together. Extend both legs out straight and as far apart as possible. Immediately squeeze the legs together with a whipping motion, keeping the ankles bent inward. Pause briefly, then repeat.

Once you have the idea, practice the frog kick with a flotation device. Glide as far as possible after each kick.

Coordinating the Body. Once you can do the hand and arm motion as well as the frog kick, then put them all together. The sequence goes like this: kick, glide, pull. The knees are drawn up for the kick at the same time that the arms are pulling. Try this for several strokes with the face in the water or completely under water.

Breathing. This stroke should be learned with the face above water at all times. Try to inhale during the arm pull phase and exhale during the kick and glide phase.

When you can do the stroke well, try it with your face in the water, going several strokes on a single breath. Then, add the breathing technique described below.

As the arms are pulling toward the feet, lift the head and take a breath. Begin exhaling immediately as you lower your face back into the water; continue to exhale as you kick and glide. You should run out of air just as you finish your glide. You may breath on every stroke or every other stroke.

SIDE STROKE

Left Arm Motion. Glide and roll the body onto the left side, keeping the left arm overhead in the glide position and placing the right arm on the right side of the body. Pull the left arm down and somewhat horizontally, toward the feet, keeping the wrist straight, palm flat, and elbow slightly bent. When it reaches the waist, lift it slightly out of the water and return it to the glide position.

Right Arm Motion. As the left arm is pulling, lift the right arm slightly out of the water, bend the elbow and draw it up toward the left hand. As the hands reach one another, the right arm enters the water. Rotate the right arm so the palm faces the feet. Straighten the elbow and push toward the feet to a full extension. The right arm should end up lying on the right side of the body, as in the initial glide.

Arm Rhythm. Both arms should be straight at the same time, and both should be bent at the same time, meeting near the waist. When the left arm reaches overhead for the glide, the right arm is on the right side of the body pointing at the feet. During the glide phase, both arms are motionless.

Scissors Kick. The side stroke uses a scissors kick, which can be learned by holding the edge of a pool, or with the hands on the bottom in shallow water, or lying on an air mattress with the legs hanging off the end.

Lie on your left side. Draw the knees up and quickly extend the legs straight out in a stride position, as if taking a long walking step. Quickly move the legs to a parallel position, moving them in a scissors-like motion, keeping the toes pointed. Once the legs are closed, take a brief pause to glide and then repeat.

Coordinating the Body. As the left arm is pulling, the knees are drawn up with the right arm. As the left arm reaches for the glide, the legs are kicked straight and scissored together. The right arm pushes toward the feet as the legs are scissoring together.

After each kick, the swimmer should glide a short way with the feet together, right arm lying along the right side of the body and the left arm in the glide position. All limbs are moving at the same time, and all limbs are motionless at the same time.

Head Position. The left ear and back of the head remain in the water, and the face remains out of the water all the time. Breathing is at will.

BACK STROKE

Glide on the back with the arms overhead and begin the flutter kick. Move one arm down, bending the elbow and keeping the wrist straight and hand flat. The arm pushes toward the feet but does not pass under the midline of the body; instead, the arm passes along the side of the body. When the hand reaches the hip, lift it completely out of the water and return it to the glide position. The arm does not move through a vertical plane but arcs more horizontally to the side. While that arm is reaching to the glide position, repeat the stroke with the other arm. The arms move alternately; when one arm is in the water, the other is out.

WHAT TO DO ABOUT CRAMPS

It is common for swimmers, especially beginners, to get muscle cramps in the leg or foot while swimming. If you don't panic, it is fairly easy to relieve any cramp that is located in the back of the thigh (hamstrings), calf, arch of the foot or toe. Simply straighten the leg, pushing the heel out and lifting the toe up. If that doesn't take care of it, place the hand on the ball of the foot and pull up, trying to straighten the leg. Then gently massage the cramped muscle and take a break. It's easy for a cramp to return if you don't take a break right away.

TREADING WATER

Without traveling, keep your body vertical and head above water by using the flutter kick and sweeping arm motions. The arms start straight out to the sides with the elbows bent a little. Move the hands toward one another, keeping the thumb side of the hands tilted up. When the hands come close together, move them back out to the sides, tilting the thumb side down. Think of smoothing sand with the hands.

The arms move back and forth smoothly and continually while the legs kick continually.

WATER GAMES AND ACTIVITIES

Most water games can be played while free swimming or on flotation devices. Inner tubes or air mattresses work well and can be used either lying down or sitting up.

Water basketball and volleyball can be played basically the same way as on land. See the Basketball and Volleyball units for variations of these games.

For water basketball, use an inner tube for a basket, or you can buy a special floating basket.

For water volleyball, stretch a net or rope above the water, held up by two uprights, as on land. For water baseball, try punchball (see the Baseball unit).

Marco Polo

Materials. One blindfold

Players. 2 or more

Object. To avoid being "It," as in Tag

To Play. One player is "It" but is blindfolded. He finds other players by calling "Marco," to which they must respond, "Polo." "It" tries to corner someone and tag him. If he does, that one becomes "It," but no one can be tagged if he is underwater.

Paddle Polo

Materials. A short-handled paddle and flotation device (such as a tube or air mattress) for each player, and a small floating ball

Players. 2 or more

Object. To score goals

To Play. Make two teams and set up a goal at each end of the playing area. Use inner tubes or stand two sticks upright just outside the pool. Players ride their floaters in an upright position, as if riding a horse. No one may touch the ball with his hands. The ball can be moved two ways:

- flinging - Tap the ball down under water. When it bounces up slip your paddle under it and balance the ball on the paddle. Then fling it where you want.

- whacking - Tap the ball down under water. When it bounces up, whack it in the air.

Players must stay on their floaters at all times, and they may go right up to the goal to shoot.

Shots and passes may be blocked, but there is to be no whacking at the ball when someone else has it.

RELAY RACES

Any of the basic strokes can be used for relay races.

SEAL

Place a ball in the water. The child must dive under and come up with his head under the ball, trying to pop it up like a seal.

SEARCH AND FIND

Children dive down after sinking objects thrown into the water. Use coins, painted stones, etc. At first, let them see where you throw them. Then, have the children close their eyes while you throw in the objects so they have to search for them.

WATER GYMNASTICS

Many gymnastic stunts can be performed in the water (see the Gymnastics unit). Try underwater front and back somersaults in the tuck, pike and straddle positions, using the hands to paddle yourself around. In shallow water, do cartwheels, headstands and handstands. From a glide, do log rolls in both directions.

In deeper water, try a back loop. Start from a back glide, then arch the back and go down head first. Keep the feet together, knees straight and toes pointed, using the hands to paddle yourself all the way around in a graceful loop.

Try handstand sculling in deep water. Come to an inverted position and scull, seeing how long you can balance. Try seeing how high you can push yourself up.

Water Tag

Water tag is played like regular tag, but in the water. See the Chase Games Unit for tag variations. Here are a few variations.

- Require all players to stay on their feet.

- Require all players to use a specified swimming stroke.

- Require all tags to be made while "It" is under water.

- Make underwater the safety zone.

CHAPTER 33

TENNIS UNIT

Tennis skills can be practiced in pairs, with or without a net, or individually, hitting the ball against a wall. With all tennis strokes, the player must try as much as possible to swing the racquet on a level plane. He must also try to hit the ball in the center of the racquet strings, lean into the stroke and have a good follow-through.

RELATED SKILLS

Handle Grip. The tennis racquet handle is gripped like any other handle, but with one difference; the index finger is moved away from the other fingers and partially hooked around the handle. This provides a little better leverage and control.

Forehand Stroke. When the ball approaches on the right side, stand sideways with the left shoulder toward the net or wall. Place the feet a little more than shoulder width apart. Draw the right arm back and swing, keeping the elbow and wrist nearly straight and firm.

Backhand Stroke. When the ball approaches on the left side, stand sideways with the right shoulder toward the net. Place the feet a little more than shoulder width apart. Cross the right arm over to the left side and swing the right arm, keeping the elbow and wrist nearly straight and firm.

Advanced Serve. Stand with the left foot in front, facing the target. Toss the ball straight up with the left hand and lean back on the right leg. Toss it only as high as you can reach with the racquet. As the ball is going up, raise your right hand behind your head, as if scratching your back with the racquet. When the ball reaches the peak of the toss, swing the racquet in a vertical plane. During the swing, extend the elbow straight and snap the wrist forward to drive the ball straight over the top of the net. Lunge forward on the left foot and have a good follow-through.

GAMES AND ACTIVITIES

TENNIS

Location. Outdoors

Players. 2 to 4

Materials. A tennis racquet for each player (a net is optional). Beginners will do better without a net

Object. To hit the ball back and forth as many times in a row as possible

To Play. If using a net, set it about waist height. One player serves, and the other tries to hit it back, keeping it going back and forth. Players may hit the ball on one bounce or before it bounces. Any time the ball hits the net and goes over, it is still in play, except on a serve. If a serve hits the net and goes over, the server gets another try.

Variation. Play without a net, just like handball (see Handball unit).

WALL TENNIS

Location. Outdoors

Players. 1 or 2

Materials. A tennis racquet for each player and a wall (garage, barn, etc.)

Object. To bounce the ball off the wall as many times in a row as possible

To Play. The ball is served to the wall. When it bounces off, the player hits it back on one bounce. With two players, take turns hitting the ball, trying to keep it going.

CHAPTER 34

TETHERBALL UNIT

No special skills are needed to play this game.

Location. Outdoors

Players.

Materials. A tetherball (a ball attached to a rope; this can be purchased at most department stores) and a pole

Object. To wrap the rope completely around the pole.

To Play. Two players stand on opposite sides of the pole. One tries to hit the ball around the pole in one direction, while the other tries to hit it in the opposite direction. The ball may be hit with the fist or open hand.

When one player succeeds, start again.

Variation. Try lowering the ball to knee level and use only the feet.

For a cooperative game, try to hit the ball back and forth from one player to the other without letting the rope wrap around the pole at all.

CHAPTER 35

TRACK AND FIELD UNIT

Track and Field events can be learned and practiced outdoors with one or more players. The events included here are those that would be practical for the typical family. The more dangerous events such as hammer, discus and javelin throwing, as well as events that require special equipment, such as pole vaulting, have been left out.

EVENTS

Shot Put - For a shot, use a heavy stone (five to fifteen pounds) according to the size and strength of the players. The player stands with his left side to the throwing line and holds the shot in his right hand, resting the hand over his right shoulder. The left arm is extended in front for balance. Bending both knees, the player leans back on the right leg and crouches. He then explosively pushes the shot as far as possible.

High Jump - Place one or two old mattresses on the ground. Have two players hold a rope horizontally while the high jumper attempts to jump over the rope without touching it and land on the mattresses. Competitive track and field requires special techniques using a one foot take-off, but at home there's no reason why players can't simply run up and dive over the rope, performing a dive roll onto the mattresses as described in the Gymnastics section of the manual. If you wish to try one of the "officially accepted" methods of high jumping, a popular one is described below in basic form, though competitive jumpers do vary on numerous points.

The Fosbury Flop. Rather than approaching the rope from straight in front, begin the run from the left side while facing the high jump area. Run in a curved pattern for eight to eleven steps. On the last step the left foot lands at about fifteen degrees to the rope, and the jumper begins to push off with the left leg. While going up, he turns his back to the rope and gains lift by vigorously driving his right knees upward and his left arm up to about head height. The jumper then thrusts the hips upward and arches slightly as his back and hips pass over the rope, and the left arm lowers to his side. Then he curls his chin to the chest and bends at the waist to whip the legs upward so they don't hit the rope as he comes down, and lands on his back.

Left-handed people would do everything to the opposite side.

Hurdles - Place a series of hurdles (obstacles, such as cardboard boxes, buckets, etc.) about 10 yards apart, for 50 to 100 yards. See how fast you can run and jump over all the hurdles without knocking any over. It helps to try to keep the lead leg and opposite arm reaching straight ahead while running over each hurdle, and to think of "running" over the hurdles, rather than "jumping" over them. Much speed is lost by jumping high over each hurdle. Instead, remain as low as possible and attempt to step over the hurdles, keeping as close as possible to normal running form.

Long Jump - Mark a "jumping line" on the ground. Have players run to the line and jump as far as they can, landing on their feet. The distance of the jump is measured from the line to the first spot that any part of the body touches the ground.

Triple Jump - This event involves traveling as far as possible using a hop, a step and a jump. Mark a "jumping line" on the ground. The jumper runs to the line and hops on one foot as far as possible, landing on the same foot. He then takes a long step, landing on the opposite foot. Last, he pushes off that foot and lands on both feet. The distance of the jump is measured from the line to the first spot that any part of the body touches the ground after the last jump.

Races - See how fast you can run various distances: 50 yards, 100 yards, 220 yards, quarter mile, half mile, one mile, two miles. For the longer runs, you need to learn to hold a steady pace and avoid exhausting yourself before finishing. Be sure to build up to these longer runs by jogging regularly for several weeks beforehand. Don't attempt the one or two-mile race unless you can already jog these distances with little difficulty.

Speed Walking. All running events can also be done with speed walking. The difference between walking and running is that when we walk, there is always one foot touching the ground. When we run, both feet are off the ground momentarily with every stride.

Baton Relays. With two or more runners you can hold a relay race that includes the extra challenge of the hand-off. You'll need some sort of a circular running track from 50 to 200 yards around, perhaps around your house. Any short stick will do for a baton, such as a twelve inch length of a broom stick. The idea is to move the baton around the track as quickly as possible with each runner carrying it for a set distance. The more efficiently you transfer the baton from one runner to the next, the better your time will be.

Make a starting line in the middle of a straight portion of the running track and line all runners up on that line. The first runner takes the baton in his left hand and goes around the track at full speed. As he approaches the starting line, the second runner begins running and reaches his right hand back to receive the baton. His hand is open wide to form an inverted V with the palm facing back. The second runner should be close to full speed before the first runner catches up to him to place the baton in the V. Once he receives the baton, he takes off at full speed, switches the baton to his left hand and repeats the hand-off with the next runner. This continues until all runners have run their portion of the race. The clock runs from the time the first runner takes off until the last runner crosses the finish line.

TRACK Meet

For a non-competitive track meet, have all players perform each event and take cumulative scores, rather than individual.

Have each player perform each event and add up all the scores to get a total team (family) score for each event but don't make a spectacle of individual scores. Then, for your next gym class, try to beat your family score.

Throwing Events. Give the first player three throws, measure each, and record his best score. After each player has had his turn, add all the recorded scores to get a total of accumulated scores. The higher the total, the better.

Jumping Events. Give the first player three jumps, measure each and record his best score. After each player has had his turn, add all the recorded scores to get a total of accumulated scores. The higher the total score, the better.

Short Running and Walking Events. For short running or walking events (up to the half mile), run as relay races (see chapter 30). For example, start the clock when the first runner begins the 100-yard dash. As soon as he finishes, the second player begins. Continue until all players have run; then stop the clock. The score is the cumulative time, and the lower the time, the better.

Long Running and Walking Events. For over a half mile, run everybody together so they don't have to wait such a long time for their turn. Tell each individual his time as he finishes and record all times. Add everyone's time together for a cumulative time; the lower the total time, the better.

High Jump. Give the first player three jumps, measure each and record his best score. After each player has had his turn, add all the recorded scores to get a total of accumulated scores. The higher the total, the better.

CHAPTER 36

VOLLEYBALL UNIT

RELATED SKILLS

Volleyball skills can be practiced outdoors, with or without a net, using any big ball that is fairly light and soft.

If you don't have an official net, you can use a clothesline rope. To make the rope easier to see, you may want to make some strips of cloth about a foot or two long and hang them about every six inches along the length of the rope.

The height of the net should be about as high as the average player can jump.

Underhand Serve. Place the left foot in front and hold the ball in the left hand at waist level. Make the right hand into a fist with the thumb to the side, the palm facing up, and the elbow nearly straight. To serve, lunge forward and strike the ball with the flat part of the fist. The ball is to be hit directly out of the hand without tossing it up. Be sure to follow through with the arm motion after the ball has been hit.

The following are the two basic skills for passing and volleying the ball when it is coming to you in the air. Emphasis should always be placed on passing the ball high in the air and nearly straight up. Low flying line drives are not good volleyball technique.

Note. Allow beginners to catch the ball, toss it up and then hit it.

Overhead Pass. (Used when the ball is high.) Look up and place the hands close together above the face. Bend the elbows and point them straight out to the sides, spread the fingers and bend the knees a little. Strike the ball with the fingertips while extending the arms straight up and straightening the knees. Follow through with the arm motion after the ball has been hit.

Underhand Pass. (Used when the ball is low.) Place one hand inside the other, bend the knees and extend the elbows almost straight. With the elbows close together, rise up by straightening the knees and strike the ball with the lower forearms. There should be little or no motion at the shoulders or elbows.

GAMES AND ACTIVITIES

VOLLEYBALL

Location. Outdoors

Players. 2 or more

Materials. One volleyball and a net

Object. To volley the ball as many times in a row as possible

To Play. Set up a team on each side of the net. One team serves, and the other volleys it back over the net on the first, second or third hit. No team may hit the ball more than three times before hitting it over the net.

When one team misses, and the ball hits the ground, whoever picks it up may serve, and all players rotate positions.

Variations

1. Try requiring everyone on a team to hit the ball before sending it over the net.

2. Try more than one ball.

3. Allow beginners to catch the ball, toss it up and hit it.

4. Try rotating players from one team to the other with each new serve.

5. Try requiring all hits to be overhead passes or underhand passes.

WALL VOLLEY

Location. In or outdoors

Players. 1 or more

Materials. One or more volleyballs

Object. To hit the ball against the wall as many times in a row as possible

To Play. Each player stands fairly close to a wall and hits his ball repeatedly against the wall. Emphasis should be on hitting the ball high on the wall. Require players to use overhead passes, underhand passes or both.

Variation. Try one ball for two players, taking turns hitting it against the wall.

BALLOON VOLLEYBALL

Location. Indoors

Players. 2 to 8

Materials. One balloon, two chairs and a piece of string

Object. To volley the balloon back and forth over the string as many times in a row as possible

To Play. Place the chairs on opposite sides of the room. Tie the string to the top of each chair to be used as the volleyball net. Volley the balloon over the string, as in volleyball.

CIRCLE VOLLEYBALL

Location. Outdoors

Players. 2 or more

Materials. One or more volleyballs

Object. To keep the ball in the air for as long as possible

To Play. Assemble players in a small circle. Pass the ball around or across the circle, using volleyball skills and trying to keep it in the air for as many hits as possible.

Variations

      1. Try as individuals to see how long one player can keep the ball up.
      2. For the very advanced, try one player keeping two balls up.

WATER BALLOON VOLLEYBALL

Location. Outdoors

Players. 2 or more

Materials. A water balloon and volleyball net

Object. To see how many times you can volley the balloon without breaking it

To Play. Played the same as Volleyball, but the balloon is caught and thrown instead of being hit.

In Closing

I hope this manual will help you in developing a complete and balanced home-school program. My only concern is that some may pursue the activities described in this manual to excess, carrying physical education beyond its rightful place. May I encourage you one last time to view physical education as something that is profitable in this life only and, even then, only when practiced in moderation. But let the spiritual disciplines be foremost in our home-school program and in each of our lives: prayer and meditation, Bible study, worship, evangelism, devotion to good deeds, Christian fellowship, etc. Let us be preoccupied with the things that make for godliness and keep physical education in the same category as brushing the teeth or personal hygiene.

> "For bodily exercise profiteth little:
> but godliness is profitable unto all things,
> having promise of the life that now is,
> and of that which is to come."
> (1 Tim. 4:8)

May God bless you as you continue to train up your children in the way they ought to go.

BIBLIOGRAPHY

Butler, Susan. *Non-Competitive Games*. Minneapolis, MN: Bethany House, 1986.

Fluegelman, Andrew. *The New Games Book*. Garden City, NY: Headlands Press, 1976.

Funk & Wagnalls New Practical Standard Dictionary, 2 vols. New York: Funk & Wagnalls, 1952. Now published at J.G. Ferguson and Assoc., Chicago, IL

Kamgberg, Mary-Lane. "Fitness for Every Body." *Current Health 2*. 17.8 (Apr. 1991): pp. 4-10.

"Infectious Diseases Awareness." *On Target*. Target and the National Federation of State High School Associations, Vol. 7, Number 5, (January 1993) p. 2.

Lynch, James M. *Steroids in Strength Training* (video). Harrisburg, PA 17108: PA Division of Health Promotion, Health and Welfare Building.

Orlick, Terry. *The Cooperative Sports & Games Book*. New York: Pantheon Books, 1978.